PAUSE

FOR INSPIRATION

in the midst of everyday life

a willing vessel
Mary

PAUSE FOR INSPIRATION in the midst of everyday life

978-0-9767485-7-1

www.PauseForInspiration.org

Published by Project Healing Press

St. Louis, Missouri

Printed in the United States of America

Edited by: JNH, a willing helper

Cover and Interior Design:
Susan Sylvia, www.StaircasePressDesign.com

PROJECT
HEALING
PRESS

Project Healing Press
St. Louis, Missouri
www.PauseForInspiration.org

ISBN: 978-0-9767485-7-1

PAUSE

FOR INSPIRATION

in the midst of everyday life

ON THE MENU:

THE **4** DECISIONS

THE 4 DECISIONS

TABLE OF CONTENTS

The 4 Decisions

The following was received from Inspiration Within as I chose to Pause, Step Back, Step Aside and Let Inspiration Guide.

I experience these words as being for the world and myself. "This Is For The Whole World" are the words that resounded in my mind as I began receiving the material for this book from Inspiration Within.

PAUSE FOR INSPIRATION™
in the midst of everyday life

THE 4 DECISIONS
PAUSE
STEP BACK
STEP ASIDE
LET INSPIRATION GUIDE

PAUSE:
The decision to stop in this moment.

STEP BACK:
The decision to get out of my own way.

STEP ASIDE:
The decision to invite Inspiration Within to help.

LET INSPIRATION GUIDE:
The decision to choose my Inspired Mind
and follow the Wisdom of Inspiration.

Apply **The 4 Decisions** *in any relationship,
activity, circumstance, situation;
pause your mind anywhere, any time.*

▶ ▶ ▶

www.PauseForInspiration.org
FREE mobile app on iTunes.

HOW TO PRACTICE THE 4 DECISIONS

1. PAUSE: The decision to stop in this moment.

I am willing: to experience my calm, quiet mind.

Action: Begin with a one moment pause. Rest. Continue pausing for as long as you choose.

2. STEP BACK: The decision to get out of my own way.

I am willing: to allow room for Another Way.

Action: Step back from feelings, thinking, planning, figuring, judging, saying and doing. No need to push them away. Allow room for Another Way. Breathe. Give some space. Let your mind be a clean slate.

3. STEP ASIDE: The decision to invite Inspiration Within to help.

I am willing: to receive Inspiration.

Action: Allow stillness to replace the chatter. Rest in Quiet patience. Be open to receiving Inspiration's Help. Put forth your questions, thoughts and/or concerns. Am I willing to ask: "Is there another way to see this?" "What will be truly helpful now?"

4. LET INSPIRATION GUIDE: The decision to choose my Inspired Mind and follow the Wisdom of Inspiration.

I am willing: to trust that there is a Wisdom and Knowing greater than what I am thinking, yet still within me, leading into an awareness of the connection to Inspiration. Inspiring a way of Being Truly Helpful in the world — now.

Action: Relax, listen and open to be Helped. Be humbly available to Inspiration. No hurry. Follow Inspiration as Inspired. No effort, no force, whenever you are willing. The choice is always yours. Inspiration's peace of mind is always ours to choose.

THE 4 DECISIONS

3

What is "Pause For Inspiration"?

Pausing for Inspiration is not a theory or a metaphor; it is a practice. It is a practice in being aware of the presence of Inspiration Within in our breathing, sleeping, waking, working, up time, down time, in the world time. It holds great potential for the one who is willing to put it into practice. Pausing for Inspiration in the midst of the mundane brings Life into life so we may experience truly living.

What is "Inspiration"?

Inspiration is The Pure Spirit of Boundless, Immense Love literally living inside each and every one of us. This Inner Present Love is our very being — the Peace we seek.

What is Your "Being"?

Your Being is who you are. You have already touched upon it several times in your life so you know to what it is I speak. It stands out, it quiets, it stills, it moves, it Inspires because it is Inspired.

Unawareness of Inspiration Within is running rampant in the world and is the cause of despair, disparaging thoughts, words and actions and simply an all around dispiritedness! Thankfully, there is an answer. The answer is Love.

What is "Love"?

The question is this:
If a child is having a nightmare, do you lock them
inside their room to bear the nightmare alone or do you
enter with the strong hand of Love to calm the fear?
When you enter with Love
a whole battalion enters with Love.
When you enter with fear, you enter alone.
Which is stronger?

Love is the epitome of who and what you are and yet, Love is so much more. Love is whom you live in and whom lives in you. Love is the Vast Nature from whom you come, the Pure Spirit in whom you live and the Door of Awareness into Love itself. It is my deepest desire that you enter into this experience for yourself! For only then is Love all Love is meant to be.

Love is the Immense Presence of Peace — Changeless, Timeless, Constant, Growing, Embracing, All-Encompassing and Eternally Grateful — grateful for you. Love is a part of everyday life in the everyday world whether we are aware of This Presence or not. Our unknowing, unwillingness, self-centeredness and unawareness have no effect on Love's Knowing, Love's Willingness, Love's Ever-Giving Nature and Love's Awareness. Such is how Love is Love. Such is how there is nowhere Love is not.

Love and the World?

Love is applicable to all situations, in all environments, relationships, conversations, discussions and actions in the world. It does not have a special place all its own — you are Love's place. Wherever you find you, there Love is. Wherever you stumble upon Love, there you are. Such is why Love is applicable and darn right useful in every circumstance of life in the world. Love heals what you thought could not be healed, loves what you thought could not be loved and raises up what you thought was dead.

Love may not give you everything you think you want or need in the world. But Love has given you YOU — and so now we may give to one another for now we truly have something to give.

Yes, even in all relationships, business, politics, social issues, the financial markets on and on, we can give to one another — yeah, Love is there all right because you are here; you are involved in these issues — right? Of course you are. If you live in this world, you are in relationships. You are a consumer of business, you are a part of the political process, you have opinions about society and the culture in which you live and you are both effected by and effect the financial markets through your everyday choices. The practice of Pause For Inspiration, The 4 Decisions addresses all of these issues because it addresses you — the cubicle you and the Inspired You.

If you live in this world, you do business in this world. It is the business of living in the world.

The cubicle mind, the mind boxed in the world, is unaware of Love, hence it is "boxed in" and has in fact boxed itself in. It has its own cubicle version of love and serves in its own way, yet this "love" is incomplete and often misses the mark. NO shame, blame or guilt; simply recognizing that the cubicle mind does not know any better because it does not know Love. There is another mind: the Mind of Inspiration Within; the Mind that is completely aware of the boxed in cubicle mind scenario, yet is not buying into its story of defeat, despair, victory over victims and utter hideousness. Whew! Glad for that.

What Will You Have Today?

Do you want to tap into the Mind of Inspiration, the Spirit of Inspiration, the Heart of Inspiration? Do you want to be a Willing Vessel of Inspiration in the world? If yes, read on because that is what this book is about. That is what the practice of "The 4 Decisions" is about — opening to Another Way. This Way is present within your Inspired Mind. All you need do is be present to Inspiration Within and be willing to Inspire the dispirited as Inspiration is Inspiring you — for you too are dispirited. Let Inspiration Guide.

Time and A Change of Mind

Time is for healing. When you realize this, and you will once you begin practicing "The 4 Decisions," life will change. Life will change because the mind living your life will have changed.

Who Is Pause For Inspiration For?
"every one and any one"

PAUSE FOR INSPIRATION is for one wanting to be drawn out of and beyond the limited nature of the cubicle self — limited because its false nature does not know you — limited because in its unknowing it is undermining what is possible for your life. More than that it is keeping you unaware of the Life of Love living inside of you — NOW.

PAUSE FOR INSPIRATION is for one willing to experience a change of mind — to grow in awareness of one's Inspired Mind.

PAUSE FOR INSPIRATION is for one who is ready to begin the sunrise of awakening to your Inspired Self. It is for one who has already begun and seeks Inspiration along the way.

PAUSE FOR INSPIRATION is helpful as well for the one who is ready to advance on their path of Inspiration. For it is in returning to the beginning again and again that one advances.

To advance is to move towards Love.

PAUSE FOR INSPIRATION is for the one who is weary and burdened and ready for rest. And even for those not yet weary of the cubicle race or not quite ready to put the brakes on just yet, but who welcomes an occasional pit stop!

As we return to the first step, the beginning, over and over again, we become aware of whereabouts we are along the path, whereabouts we are not — that we are not as far along and advanced as we may have thought — for that matter, not as far along and advanced as our *thinking*, and the eventual realization that we do not care nor need to know whereabouts we are on the path —

For the path has become indistinguishable from life itself.

If you want to advance however, begin again; the first step is the step to advancement for it is the beginning from which all follows.

What Is The First Step, the Beginning?

Willingness. Rest willingly towards Inspiration Within, saying "Here I am."

This Book Is An Offering To You

If you do nothing with this book after reading it, that will be fine, as it will have done something worthwhile within you. And this you will take with you wherever you go. It is a message without pompous appeal, mass appeal or worldly appeal. Certainty seldom reveals itself to those who do not want to hear it. Love is Certainty. The choice to hear is always ours.

If you take nothing more from this book than the practice of "The 4 Decisions," you take it all. For it is in this practice that one moves from doing to being, from being a doer in the world, to doing in the world from one's *being*. This practice leads one into *being* an embodiment of Inspiration Within. How? Firstly, by accepting that Love loves you and allowing yourself to receive This Love — every moment you choose to Pause For Inspiration. Secondly, by practicing choosing Inspiration, present within one's True Self, anytime, anywhere. Thirdly, by giving Inspiration away — sharing Inspiration in your homes, on your job, with family, friends, your community, the world and yes, even on the streets where you are moving about day in and day out — literally! How? In your being willing to be an instrument of The Inspiration that is within you.

What Are You Waiting For?

The world to change without you changing? Your life to change without you beginning to choose to think, see, hear, touch and live differently? Inspiration is ready when you are willing.

Do not decide now whether or not to read this book. Ask within if it may be worthwhile to go through the practice of "The 4 Decisions" which will bring you into awareness of your Inspired Mind. Open to this experience, moving from an outer focus to an inner focus, and listen for the prompting of Inspiration Within.

The 4 Decisions

The 4 Decisions brings to light your ongoing relationship and communication with Inspiration Within — a way of being in touch all throughout the day with this Inner Present Love, who loves, so now we can love. We can attempt to compartmentalize this Inner Present Love into our special times, special groupings, special relationships and special "needs" and desires OR we can let This Love be expressed through us day in and day out in the midst of the mundane. It is in the ordinariness of life that Inspiration is available to us in ways seen and unseen.

It is our life opportunity to pay attention and to be willing living vessels of the Extraordinary in the ordinary.

There is power in the ordinary circumstances of life; they are to be lived, not tolerated; we are to *be with* all of it, not rush to the rest of it. So even while you are planning out your day, your life, your next endeavor, consider: Pausing, Stepping Back, Stepping Aside and Letting Inspiration Guide.

Giving a Moment Now to Practicing The 4 Decisions

Mary Sharing

The 4 Decisions are a message, an Inspired Message. The phrase, "Pause, Step Back, Step Aside and Let Inspiration Guide," showed up in the beginning of the listening within and writing of this book. Over three years later someone asked, "What does "Pause, Step Back, Step Aside and Let Inspiration Guide" mean? I did not want to give this person an off-the-top-of-my-cubicle-head answer so I decided to Pause, Step Back, Step Aside and Let Inspiration Guide! I asked Inspiration Within, "What does this phrase mean?" I heard from within, "They are each a decision." Then I was Given The 4 Decisions. Here they are.

Suggestion: The 4 Decisions is specific in that they are here to potentially bring you help with any activity, relationship, circumstance or situation; pause your mind, anywhere, any time. In fact, you need not have a specific reason to practice The 4 Decisions other than to experience peace. So, you may begin your practice with the thought of something you would like help with. If nothing comes to you right now, practice The 4 Decisions simply to receive peace into your mind. You have nothing to lose. At the very least, you may experience helpful, simple relaxation!

PAUSE
FOR INSPIRATION
in the midst of everyday life

PRACTICE THE 4 DECISIONS
in any relationship, activity, circumstance, situation

HOW TO PRACTICE THE 4 DECISIONS

1. PAUSE:
The decision to stop in this moment.
I am willing: to experience my calm, quiet mind.
Action: Begin with a one moment pause. Rest. Continue pausing for as long as you choose.

2. STEP BACK:
The decision to get out of my own way.
I am willing: to allow room for Another Way.
Action: Step back from feelings, thinking, planning, figuring, judging, saying and doing. No need to push them away. Allow room for Another Way. Breathe. Give some space. Let your mind be a clean slate.

3. STEP ASIDE:
The decision to invite Inspiration Within to help.
I am willing: to receive Inspiration.
Action: Allow stillness to replace the chatter. Rest in Quiet patience. Be open to receiving Inspiration's Help. Put forth your questions, thoughts and/or concerns. Am I willing to ask: "Is there another way to see this?" "What will be truly helpful now?"

4. LET INSPIRATION GUIDE:
The decision to choose my Inspired Mind and follow the Wisdom of Inspiration.
I am willing: to trust that there is a Wisdom and Knowing greater than what I am thinking, yet still within me, leading into an awareness of the connection to Inspiration. Inspiring a way of Being Truly Helpful in the world — now.
Action: Relax, listen and open to be Helped. Be humbly available to Inspiration. No hurry. Follow Inspiration as Inspired. No effort, no force, whenever you are willing. The choice is always yours. Inspiration's peace of mind is always ours to choose.

A LOOK AT EACH OF THE 4 DECISIONS

1 Pause: The decision to stop in this moment.

What does this mean? To pause is to come into awareness that you are not pausing. You heard right! On and on you go and rarely if ever do you notice: "on and on you go." To where on and on are you going? To whom do you attribute this ongoing-ness? When you stop to reflect on your ongoing-ness, how do you feel? Who is it that is going on and on and is compelled to do so? By the way, this does not necessarily only refer to keeping busy in our lives; one may be going on and on in one's mind — as is the state of affairs of the cubicle mind.

Be not afraid. Do not fear pausing from your self a moment. Enjoy a break from whomever it is that is doing all of this ongoing-ness. Do not worry, you can return again and again to this cubicle self who is in inconsistent ongoing-ness — and you will inevitably do so. Inconsistent ongoing-ness? Yes. The nature of the cubicle self is inherently inconsistent and not to be confused, even in its better moments, with our True Nature — our Inspired Self. Yet, we look to it as if it is our true nature and the true nature of others and when it does not demonstrate consistency we get frustrated. The error is relying on that which is inconsistent when all the while we can rely on Inspiration Within to consistently supply what is Truly Helpful. The choice is ours. For example, it would not be helpful to keep a can opener that only opens cans on Tuesdays and Fridays. A can opener that consistently functions as a can opener is best. Yet, you value this inconsistency within yourself because you depend on it for "sustenance!" Imagine that.

Pausing brings great relief

I AM WILLING TO EXPERIENCE MY CALM, QUIET MIND

Rest. You have a calling to which you must respond —
eventually. It is the calling of Inspiration Within. You will
hear such a calling in the Inner Quiet and it will calm you.

ACTION: BEGIN WITH A ONE MOMENT PAUSE. REST.
CONTINUE PAUSING FOR AS LONG AS YOU CHOOSE.

BEGIN WITH A ONE MOMENT PAUSE

Pausing is resetting your life. Resetting the way you think
about life; resetting the way you see. To reset is to begin
again. Everyone deserves a second chance. You are
given more than two chances; every moment is an
opportunity to begin again. Pause.

REST

Rest.

Resting is an act of Love in you. Rest this restless, anxiety-
ridden cubicle mind. The body will follow. The body begins
with the mind, thus changing out the mind that is running
the body down to a rattled, wound up, shredded thread,
will help. Relieve this restless self of itself. Receive a
replenishing afternoon nap in any true moment — the
moment of pause. The best functioning mind is the mind
at rest. Let Inspiration Within rest your restless mind.

CONTINUE PAUSING FOR AS LONG AS YOU CHOOSE

Choose the pause and be in the pause. Sometimes the
pause chooses you. Let yourself be chosen — ah. In your
pausing you pause to another and you begin a domino
effect of the pause all throughout. No need to have to
reside in a special place — pause where you find your
self and find your True Self in the pause. Pause indeed for
as long as you like, wherever you like. Relish the pause.
Relinquish the fear.

2 Step Back: The decision to get out of my own way.

What does this mean? How does one get out of the way? First, by being willing to see that you — this "me" character is in the way. In the way of what? In the way of your aware-ness of the Inspired You who is not this dispirited you who is this "me." "Me" is on the attack, mainly upon one's self, but often towards others — the two seem to go hand in hand. To be in one's own way is the supreme example of launching an attack on one's self. You may think you are forging ahead at what is right for you or someone else. All the while you are actually attacking yourself. Though you may appear to be doing something of great value, your lack of attention to your greater value is causing you great suffering beneath the appearances. How does one know one is suffering beneath appearances? Unfortunately, most do not know precisely because they do not want to know.

I AM WILLING TO ALLOW ROOM FOR ANOTHER WAY

There is Another Way. Hopefully, for you, all of us and for the world, you are open and willing to see another way. For those who seek more than the coming and going of worldly satisfaction, something more to live for than personal achievement, there lays within them a palace of delight in whom one will find their Inspired Self. Not a magical thought, but your True Delightful Self. A Self who is not weary, arrogant or unbeknownst, but a Self who is living in meaning, exuberance and in whom one finds hope.

Hope is experiencing that all is well right now — not because of something spectacular that you have accomplished in your past or have yet to accomplish, rather because of the Something Spectacular that is accomplishing itself in you.

Fear not about getting out of your own way. Resting behind your own way is a way that is beyond you, yet truly is you. It is the way the world knows not of, though wrestles in its trying. Yet, you can give up trying. Go ahead, give up. Give up what has been deluding you. Give up what has offered nothing but shambles in the end. Give up what is not your daily sustenance. Give up what is not being of service to yourself and others. Give up nothing, for it is nothing. Be thankful for this nothing you give up for it is in your giving it up that you come upon what has been Given you that you cannot give yourself — You. You are a *being* that has been Given much and has much to give in all you have been Given. There are no losses in your giving for this Love you give is not of your own making, thus you have nothing to lose.

What is it that one is to step back from exactly? Most do not understand this self they have made, thus to ask you to step back from it is perplexing. Inspiration Within will help you. Inspiration helps you by teaching you what exactly it is you are to step back from. Yes, exactly. Exactly in that you will receive teaching that is best suited for you at the time with each and every circumstance you find yourself facing. The prescription is written and dispensed exactly for you. Follow the directions. Inspiration Within, your Inner Teacher, knows best because Inspiration knows you. Listen. Experience what it is to truly be known.

ACTION: STEP BACK FROM FEELINGS, THINKING, PLANNING, FIGURING, JUDGING, SAYING AND DOING

What does this mean? It is possible to function without the constant chatter of feeling, thinking, planning, figuring, judging, saying and doing. It is not the implication to exclude all of these. The guidance is to be Inspired in the midst of all of these functions. Receive Inspiration in the middle of your feeling, thinking, planning, figuring, judging, saying and doing.

Be aware of the continual presence of Inspiration Within throughout the day in your pausing.

No need to question your every feeling, thought... Simply rest with This Presence and watch how your feelings, thoughts, planning, figuring, judging, saying and doing shift. Shift in a way to serve you so you are now able to be in the service of yourself and others. It will become transparent that Inspiration Within is giving you a better way in your willingness to get out of your own way.

AND THE BOAT WHISPERED

There will be experiences of unrest in all this as it is appropriate that the old ways of being shall resist and experiencing strain is to be expected.

Imagine a boat ready to set sail and how the tattered rope that has been keeping it tied to the shore efforts to do its job. Not realizing its job has come to its finish, the rope is busy holding on, pulling, yanking, wearying itself, tearing itself apart, unraveling, giving it one last good shot, coming back for another round in an attempt to keep its job or do a better job; all the while the boat whispers to the rope, "It is finished." Your old ways are the rope. You are the boat. Set sail.

VALUING THE ROPE

You value the rope. How is it that you are pulled back over and over again into seeing yourself, your life and your relationships — and even the world — as nothing more than a tattered, old rope to be saved and hidden away or treasured and delegated great stature — a place in the crowd. What is your valuing of the rope bringing into your life and the lives of others? Where does your heart go to rest?

Let's look at how you value the rope. The second of The 4 Decisions asks you to step back from: feelings, thinking, planning, figuring, judging, saying and doing.

FEELINGS

Your strongest urges are seen in how you feel. Making one's feelings the authority over life and day-to-day decisions is a path that puts many stones in your way. All paths in this world have stones or they would not be paths. In and of themselves, stones are not bad. Stones are natural on the path of human life experience. Some feelings feel like huge stones in your path. They seem to bounce up and hit you, or another, right between the eyes. They appear around your feet making it difficult to move. Not to worry. There is another way.

Fretting over stones in one's path is like wishing fruit did not have seeds. Seeds have value in that they bring forth the fruit. Feelings have value. Turning them over to Inspiration Within reveals their true value for then what lies beneath the feelings comes to the surface — into conscious aware-ness. Seeds give rise to fruit. Feelings given to Inspiration Within give rise to awareness. Feelings are not to be removed from our consciousness, rather noted and felt, like the passing of an inner breath and relinquished so a new breath may come into being. Nothing more, nothing less are feelings.

THINKING

Stepping back from thinking appears to be nonsense. However, Inspiration is not thinking what you are thinking when Inspiration says, "step back from thinking." To step back is to first notice what it is I am stepping into. Notice how you step forth in your mind without pausing to see whereabouts you are headed. What is it that draws you into certain thinking that holds no future for you? No real, true future anyway. Is it valuable to hinder one's truthful, Inspired thoughts arising from Inner Present Love in favor of self-hatred, dismay and despair? Surely not, yet it happens all of the time.

Ask yourself hourly or whenever you choose to remember, "Am I here to share peace or commit to the ongoing pain of myself and my fellow travelers here in this world, on this earth?" Is it not worth a moment of your preciousness to humble yourself to peace? All that will be humbled is the hatred and unworthiness you carry on your back and ask others to carry for you. Let it go.

PLANNING

Our greatest fears are planned. Cubicle plans come forth from fear, meanwhile Love is loving. I hear you. This seems absurd I know! Yet, it is true. Cubicle plans are afraid — afraid that its plans will not go as planned! Looking ahead at how to behave, what to wear, who to be, who not to be, who to talk to, who not to talk to, what to say, what not to say — keeping the lid on tight and the cubicle walls upright! Whereas, an Inspired Outlook prepares you for what has not yet happened. Inspiration Within prepares you in its loving you. Now you are prepared — prepared to love within the context of your daily plan.

The cubicle mind will have you thinking that if your life is not exactly planned according to its measure, you will miss out. Who is it that is missing out? Missing out on what exactly? The cubicle mind engages in attacking one's self with plans to stay in control as an attempt to ward off feelings of unworthiness. Ironically, not planning can also be caused by unworthiness. So, what are you to do? Plan or not plan? Look inside and see what is going on behind your planning.

Wisdom planning is a whole different kind of planning. This is planning with your Inspired Mind. What is it that your Inspired Mind is calling you forth to plan, to participate in and to begin? The good news is that cubicle planning will not reveal your untouched worthiness; trusting an Inspired Plan will.

Does this mean you are not to make appointments, set goals, prepare for meetings and have schedules? Yes? No? It means to choose to be aware of Inspiration's presence in the midst of it all. Plan away. Just don't plan your life away without pausing for Inspiration.

FIGURING

Figuring is the belief that calculating will protect me from harm. Figure your accounts, figure those measurements, but look at what is often the motivation behind all of the figuring going on in your mind. Worry! Worry is the motivation for most figuring. Worry is mistakenly viewed as a way to protect your self from harm. This is caused by the suffering coming from experiencing yourself as being unsafe — in harm's way. Such suffering is bleeding over the earth. What is the answer?

Physical world lack of safety is a given. Bodies are vulnerable to physical attack in the world. Inspiration Within is invulnerable to attack. Go ahead and figure how to protect your body, but do not expect it to protect your mind. All safety begins in the mind. A mind at peace is a mind that is safe. As feelings of vulnerability arise, be open to Inspiration living inside of you — lean into Love. You have access to a mind that was not composed by fear, but by Love. Let this be the mind, your Inspired Mind, doing any required figuring. The Mind of Inspiration is clear and will bring clarity into your awareness.

JUDGING

Back away. Choose to see. Draw no conclusions just yet. Let this moment be free of your opinions, sizing up and down of another or condemnation of a person, relationship or situation. Pause. Pause from assessing, evaluating and managing.

Judgment is a necessary tool in your world. It is a tool used to see or remain blind to that which you do not want to see. Judgment is necessary to take action or to decide against taking action; to speak forth or decide not to speak. Judgment can be used to see that one needs to build a fire for warmth or it can be used to destroy a nation. You judge. You choose.

The question is: Who is it who is judging? The self-absorbed, self-centered mind or the mind aware of Love — the Inspired Heart∞Mind? The self-centered self generally comes bolting into our awareness first and because it is first we often mistakenly think it is the thought to follow. In pausing and stepping back, awareness of Inspiration Within enters into one's mind and now there is another way of seeing, another way of judging. Inspiration is the big picture through which relationships can now be seen. Inspiration is the big picture — now we can see through new eyes.

Judgment is a tool to assess everyday scenarios with which we believe we are fully capable of assessing without the help of Inspiration Within just because we are familiar with the scene. Is it possible that your familiarity with the situation, activity or relationship is influencing the way you are seeing and this is an obstacle to allowing something greater, something more helpful to enter?

Judgment is a tool used to plan and evaluate a plan, to make decisions about all kinds of things we label as small

or big. If you were to devise a plan from the perspective of your Inspired Mind, might it be a plan that serves an Inspired purpose? How are you to know how a seemingly small decision may affect the rest of your life or how a seemingly big "personal" or "business" or "financial" or "social justice" or "political" decision will affect the lives of countless others. This is the point, you do not know everything and you are not expected to know everything.
So chill.

Will it hurt to pause and step back out of your own cubicle mind and open to another way? A way that may save you and/or others hours of time, years of struggle, relationship turmoil, health problems, untold amounts of money, pain and suffering… a way that may even save one life or many lives, a way that may save others from loneliness, rejection and despair. A way that may not be the ideal plan for how you want your life to unfold, but a way that is unfolding inside of you and has a way of living already thought out for you that is perfect for you because the plan actually IS YOU! Your Inspired Self is the plan! It is the plan for you, your family and friends, your co-workers, your neighborhood, community, relationships and the world. Inspiration is awakening you to your True, Inspired Self. I know you may be judging this as pure poppycock. Here is the offer. Go ahead and continue along your road to success or mission incomplete — or, if you are not afraid of true success, of completing an Inspired mission, pause and step back from judging.

Do not be confused. You are confused if you start thinking ahead and judging what this all means because you do not know what is in store for you. Cubicle judgment will delay an Inspired Plan for your life. Period. That is okay — to delay is not to nullify. **The question is:** "Do you want to delay?"

Inspired plans do not come down the pipe without a willing receptacle to deposit them upon. Take the lid off of your judgmental mind and receive. Judging fear, how fear is playing out in your self, your relationships and in the world, is not the answer to the fear. Being willing to be Inspired is the answer to all fear.

Most judgment is around feeling that someone has mistreated you or offended you and now you sit in judgment of this one. Or you do not like the way someone dresses, talks or behaves and you judge them as unworthy for not being like you. The central theme is seeing through the eyes of "difference." How is this person different from "me"—here is this me-character again—and how is "me" better or worse? **You have a choice:** judge or forgive.

To forgive is to see —
To see truly.
To see with eyes knowing how to see.
Because these eyes
Know Love.

Judge not in another for that which you would want forgiveness. For this type of judgment to befall another is bondage for both parties.

Forgive as you want to be forgiven. What about consequences and punishment for words and actions that are hateful and cause harm? Forgiveness does not undo the worldly consequences and punishment that one must face. Real forgiveness however, lets yourself and/or another know inside that even though you or another may have missed the mark, who one truly is, one's very being, is not undone, but awaits your recognition.

Judgment and consequences
are necessary for a society to function.
Forgiveness is necessary
for Inspiration to function in the world.

SAYING

What holds greater value to you: saying what is on your mind or minding what is on your mind before it works its way to your lips? The words spoken over another or yourself can either be the kiss of death or the wisdom of Life. Your words proclaim the belief in death or Life. Impale the spell of death or infuse awareness of Life into someone.

You may not realize how you are misusing words or the sound of your words or laughter. Some part of you knows. You are afraid; this is why you speak harsh words, unhelpful words, limiting words, sarcastic words, damning words, belittling words over another. Look at the fear. Allow Inspiration Within to show you what is going on inside of you that is causing you to project your fear onto another. Avoiding fear will not serve you and will prohibit you from serving yourself and others. In avoiding that within you that is not serving yourself and others, you will not be served.

It is no little thing, this placing value on demeaning words, sarcastic laughter or whatever other accusatory or questioning sound makes its way out of your cubicle self. It is a big thing. It is a statement coming from lack. You experience yourself as lacking — lacking Love. You are not lacking in Love and Love is not lacking in you. Your unawareness of the abundance of Love within you, within another, is the lack you feel. Call upon Inspiration Within. Draw from This Abundance as you are speaking and speak This Abundance over others.

DOING

Inspired doing is to act with enthusiasm and fortitude that comes from *Love*; all other doing is self-fabrication. Yes, it is true. Even doing the dishes in your own strength is to believe that the self you made up is more powerful and valuable than the Self you have been given. May sound extreme, but it is not. Do not be disturbed by this teaching. Relax into it! Give thanks that you are not required to operate in this world by your own strength. It is not that you do not have strength, for you do, thus to rely on something you call "strength" that you have mustered up all by your lonesome, is not your real strength. Strong are those who allow themselves to receive Help.

Do not rest on your laurels. Rest in the pause. The worth-whileness of the doing that will come forth from stepping back from doing on your own will someday be seen. Trust what is unseen in this moment and you will one day rejoice in what you see.

NO NEED TO PUSH THEM AWAY. ALLOW ROOM FOR ANOTHER WAY.

Your feelings, thinking, planning, figuring, judging, saying and doing need not be pushed out of your awareness as if pretending they are not there. Fear pushes away.

Inspiration draws you close. In drawing you close, Inspiration will gladly take from you all that you choose to give it in exchange for another way — a peace-filled way.

> Better to have a bad day and eventually
> Come into the presence of Inspiration Within
> Than to have a good day all on your own.

BREATHE

The breath of Inspiration is clear and clears —
This Peace is breathing in you — breathe in This Peace.

GIVE SOME SPACE

Giving some space happens in your stepping back from yourself and all that is happening in your mind. Spaciousness enters and lightens the load.

LET YOUR MIND BE A CLEAN SLATE

Your world is not going to suddenly fall apart if you take a moment or two and allow awareness to spread out a fresh, clean, open space upon which you may take a seat. Be here.

This leads straight into the third decision.

3 Step Aside: The decision to invite Inspiration Within to help.

What? You have already stepped back, now you have to step aside, too? Yes. Be not afraid. Stepping aside is putting out the welcome mat for Inspiration Within. You have a part in all of this. Your part has been perfectly created and crafted within you — it is your exquisite willingness to allow Inspiration to be Inspiration. It is your willingness to be host to Inspiration. Receive your Guest. Being host to Inspiration Within, you will come to see within yourself a well-mastered place; *a place that dwells in service to you and to those you serve. Be the host.*

I AM WILLING TO RECEIVE INSPIRATION

Opening to Inspiration Within *is willingness.* There is nothing you need to make happen. Simply be willing. In willingness your whole being comes into Inspired Alertness, a restful, awakened state. Your slumbering replaced with a purposeful decision to receive Inspiration. Unfold any clenching — open. Seeing your cares and woes absorbed into peace — Now your hands are empty — receive.

ACTION: Allow stillness to replace the chatter. Rest in Quiet patience. Be open to receiving Inspiration's Help. Put forth your questions, thoughts and/or concerns. Am I willing to ask: "Is there another way to see this?" "What will be truly helpful now?"

ALLOW STILLNESS TO REPLACE THE CHATTER

Allow sanity to replace insanity. Give pardon to the cubicle conversation being carried on in your mind; and I mean carried — what a load. Drop it. In your stepping aside you are now the host to stillness. Opening to the stillness between the words and behind the thoughts of any residual chatter. Stillness abounds.

THE 4 DECISIONS

REST IN QUIET PATIENCE

Patience is not something the cubicle mind understands. It boxes patience up within its time frame. Okay, it says, I will be patient for 5 minutes, but that's all! The cubicle self is incapable of patience, real patience. So the direction to "Rest in Quiet patience" is given. Unrest is the nature of the noisy cubicle mind, thus it lacks patience. Rest is the nature of Quiet. Be with Quiet. Find patience here.

BE OPEN TO RECEIVING INSPIRATION'S HELP

Open how? Pause. Pausing is opening. You may hear a lot about being open, opening ourselves up etc. The cubicle self does not know how to truly open. It is closed for business when it comes to opening to Inspiration! Be opened and open.

How does Inspiration Within help? By coming to your aid illuminating any lingering darkness in your mind. Darkness is the experience of forgetting the light is on. Choosing the mind in the dark is like walking into a light-filled room with your eyes closed, feeling around for your closet and look- ing for your white shirt. Hmm. And why would you not use the light that is fully at your disposal? Being open is flipping your awareness switch ON. The light of Inspiration is always at your disposal. It is always on. If you want to be aware of this fact, pause.

Illuminating the darkness clears up a lot of confusion for now you are not rumbling around in your dark closet, fall- ing into the closet, knocking things over, getting hit on the head by junk falling out of the closet, tripping over the stuff falling at your feet, busting your toe on the edge of the fur- niture as you walk out with what you are guessing is your white shirt only to eventually see that you grabbed the wrong shirt, in fact, it's not even a shirt, it's a pajama top… on and on and such a waste of time. Open instead?

Inspiration Within sees all that needs to be seen and helps you see it too. Even if your vision is not so clear just yet after opening to Inspiration's help, you have been Given an inner flashlight, your Inspired Heart∞Mind, to lead you through the darkness. This is the Heart∞Mind with the light on.

PUT FORTH YOUR QUESTIONS, THOUGHTS AND/OR CONCERNS.

Inspiration Within your Inspired Heart∞Mind will take anything you are willing to give! It is an Inner Knowing calling out, "Questions, thoughts, concerns? I am here to help." The only thing is, this Inner Knowing is not selling anything, rather, offering you free help. How many times do you disregard this Inner Knowing, thinking there is nothing there for you? You are hungry for something else. And just what "something else" would that be? What are you hungry for? Thirsting for? Love is here with Real Help! And it is free! No strings attached. Receive it!

Deprive yourself of receiving help and you deprive another as well. For it is in your receiving help that you will now be able to help another. How long do you intend to listen to this monotonous voice yelling out, "No, I'm okay, everything's fine, I don't really have any problems I need help with right now. I can figure this one out on my own. This practice isn't for me, maybe I will tell so and so about this or maybe I'll give it a whirl sometime down the line when I need some help; in other words, "when things in my life are really falling apart." Are you kidding? Face it. You know all about falling apart or you would not be reading this.

Your cubicle blind thinking needs healing,
not new sunglasses!

The body's eyes may have 20/20 vision, but the thinking of the cubicle self is short-sighted, blind-sighted and has been sighted looking everywhere for nothing and finding it!

The cubicle mind is falling apart! Look around you. Look inside of you. People, the world, your friends, your family, your neighbors, you — are falling apart! Look within you, surely something in you is crying out for help or something in you wants to help, but does not know how to begin.

Herein lies the problem. Your unwillingness to ask for help and receive help is causing your unawareness of needing help and needing to help others. You have received a Great Gift and yet you refuse over and over again to open the Gift.

Your constant decision to delay your opening of this Gift is leading you nowhere; meanwhile all of Love awaits you. Help is at your doorstep. You will have the opportunity to receive this help or turn it away; each choice is this choice. You will remain uncertain about this choice as long as you remain unwilling to receive help.

What then are you to give to Inspiration Within in order to receive help in return? This moment will do. Give this moment to Inspiration Within.

Give all that appears to be happening within you, to you, to another, in front of you, ahead of you, in your sight, out of sight, in your mind, in your heart, in your past, in your future, today, tomorrow, yesterday, history, time, space, body, mental state, emotional state, relationships, hatred, love, evil, darkness, light, prayer, government, politics, voting, current events, entertainment, a decision, a worry, a thought, a feeling, a grievance, jealousy, greed, envy, lying, gossip, playing, sports, arts, music, dance, poetry, writing, emailing, phone calling, conversations, unforgiveness, discussions, sharing, giving, receiving, reading, watching television, movies, hobbies, instincts, intuitions, awareness, fitness level, routine, brain work, healing, health, jargon, intellect, appointments, bank accounts, kitchen work, laundry, running errands, raising children, caregiving for your parents, sleeping, waking, being a helper in the world and anything else!

Anything else?

You need Love's Help with everything IF you want the Healing Peace that only Love gives.

AM I WILLING TO ASK, "IS THERE ANOTHER WAY TO SEE THIS?" "WHAT WILL BE TRULY HELPFUL NOW?"

Are you willing to ask? It is up to you. Ask anything. Here is the deal: If you are not willing to give over any of this stuff renewing its lease on your mind and taking up residence in your heart and body, you are forfeiting the help. Yes, Inspiration Within is forever standing at the intersection of willingness and unwillingness. Which will you choose? As for your questions, the answers are Given as your questions are given to Inspiration Within. All questions, thoughts and concerns receive a Response — not necessarily in the timing you want, but in the way you need.

THE DUST SETTLES

Stepping Aside settles the dust.

Breathe.

4 Let Inspiration Guide: The decision to choose my Inspired Mind and follow the Wisdom of Inspiration.

A choice is upon you. Decide for or against Love, for or against Joy, for or against Hope. Your choosing to continue lollygagging along, ordering your every moment and forgetting all about Inspiration is the choice to forget who you are. The decision to follow Wisdom is the choice for your True Self. You are free to choose and you are choosing every moment. Do you want to know who you are? Follow.

To follow Wisdom is to be Wise. Contrary to cubicle belief, following is not passive or apathetic. The Inspired Strength inside of you becomes useful when you follow Inspiration Within. You are always choosing and trusting. You follow whatever or whomever you choose and trust. Choose and trust wisely. The intricate details of the path ahead of you — exactly where you are being led — may not be known to you — this is actually helpful because if you knew too much about the trip, you would start planning it!

The Wisdom of Inspiration is *being held* in you. Following this Wisdom *is* choosing your Inspired Mind for this Wisdom communicates with you through your Inspired Mind. Following this Wisdom is choosing who you truly are! Wisdom about everything, from doing the laundry to your health to your relationships, your work and all other matters. Do not be afraid. Follow the Wisdom Within; you will never be given more Wisdom than you can handle in any given moment!

I AM WILLING TO TRUST THAT THERE IS A WISDOM AND KNOWING GREATER THAN WHAT I AM THINKING, YET STILL WITHIN ME, LEADING INTO AN AWARENESS OF THE CONNECTION TO INSPIRATION. INSPIRING A WAY OF BEING TRULY HELPFUL IN THE WORLD — NOW.

TRUST

Trust is the recognition that there is Something Greater within me who knows who I truly am and contrary to all cubicle evidence telling me that I am something other than who I truly am, This Something still loves me. As you trust this Knowing, your constant journey of self-reliance is coming to an end. Cubicle self-reliance is highly over-rated. Your cubicle reasoning and doubt are holding you in distrust. Another way awaits you — the way of trust. Your worldly responsibilities will still be accomplished — no worries. Trust Inspiration who lives in full acceptance of who you truly are and offers only mercy in those times that we venture away. How does one practice trusting?

Lean into Love.

Trusting Wisdom moment-to-moment draws an end to inner conflict moment-to-moment. Conflict is the result of drifting away from your Inspired Mind and drifting into your cubicle mind. What are you conflicted about? One reason you experience conflict is because of your lack of trust in Inspiration Within and holding on to cubicle thinking.

Trust is the key to establishing a relationship with Inspiration. No cubicle reasoning will undo your lack of trust no matter how sound it may sound. Wisdom will undo your lack of trust if you are willing to have it undone.

Here It Is

You distrust Inspiration Within because you have
forgotten the "Within" part.
You believe in an Inspiring Love, or not,
that is somehow on the outside –
somewhere outside of you waiting to rain down on your
head.
That is untruth.
The truth is that
Love lives inside of you.
Believe this, or do not believe this.

The fact is, in this life
you will either come to hate/fear Love because you have
not been willing to come to know Love
OR
You will be indifferent towards Love
Which is the same as hate/fear
OR
you will come to Love.

Only in your experience of truly resonating with Inspiration Within will you experience your complete trust in it; even then you will fall from trust from time to time. Be not afraid. Until you have this experience, trust is still available to you — through gratitude. Gratitude has a way of deepening our trust in Inspiration Within. Expressing gratitude within or to another, is acknowledging the reality and power of Inspiration in your everyday life. Gratitude is opening to an experience of seeing Inspiration at work in the here and now — in the ordinariness of life.

Practice gratitude to increase trust.

WISDOM AND KNOWING

But what is this Wisdom from Inspiration Within that you are being asked to choose, trust and follow — because that is a tall order. Truly I tell you, the taller order is your little willingness and it is this that must precede your choosing, trusting and following. Great is your willingness to trust the cubicle self who offers you nothing of real value. Hence, now it should be easy for you to offer that which I ask of you — a little willingness. Little willingness is what is asked of you. The "Pause" is such willingness. Pausing is a great accomplishment for in it you will see. This is Wisdom.

Elder years do not accomplish this Wisdom for many are elderly and unwise. To experience this Wisdom is to experience your True Self. Unknowing is the cubicle self of this Wisdom because it knows not of the Voice from which it comes. It listens to another voice.

This Wisdom, not of the world, is operating fully in the

world — listen closely. Only you can come into an experience of Wisdom for yourself. There is nothing to fear. This Knowing is not separate from you and your life. You are inextricably connected. You will see This Knowing and know it is real.

Pause, be willing and ask
This Wise Knower to reveal itself within you now.

GREATER THAN WHAT I AM THINKING

Did you pause? How can you trust what is greater than what you are thinking? You manage to trust your own thinking day in and day out. Take no offense to this statement. "Me" gets offended. Who is it that is thinking that this me-thinking is reliable? What if you were to trust This Unlimited Wisdom Within who knew you before you knew of yourself? How about trusting this Big Picture Knowing who is reliable in seeing the Whole. Defend your cubicle thinking and you will have to return to "Step Back, the decision to get out of my own way." Cubicle thinking is not bad thinking; it may often sound quite "wise" and intelligent.

*Cubicle thinking is always in part
because it is generated from the experience of
"being apart."*

You are so much more than your cubicle thinking and Wisdom knows that about you and knows the you who is beyond your thinking. Think with Inspiration. Now, that is an Inspired Thought.

YET STILL WITHIN ME

You are not outside of This Knowing nor is This Wisdom outside of you. If Knowing were on the outside it would not be Knowing; the Whole Nature of Knowing is that it rises up on the inside of you — let it. If Knowing were on the outside, you could not ever come to see that you are known, nor could you ever come to know. Knowing *is* the Inside Track — You are on the Inside Track.

AWARENESS

Awareness is beyond thought. Awareness is being present to this All-Encompassing Love who cannot be overshadowed, cannot be overcome. In This Love's being aware of you, now you can be aware.

CONNECTION TO INSPIRATION

You and Inspiration Within, these seeming "two," are in truth connected as one. This oneness is the inner freedom you long for.

INSPIRING A WAY OF BEING TRULY HELPFUL IN THE WORLD — NOW.

You are in this world to Be Truly Helpful. A way of Being Truly Helpful is available to you 24/7. Thinking unhelpful, fear-based thoughts is unhelpful to yourself and everyone. It can be different. Choosing to think with Inspiration is in the realm of possibility.

To Be Truly Helpful is to live forth from an Inspired Heart∞Mind. Damage or harm coming to another is always the result of someone being trapped in a cubicle mindset — the mindset of aloneness, separation, isolation and fear.

Error occurs when you choose the cubicle mind. Right thinking is Inspired Thinking. How you think about someone or some situation or relationship is Truly Helpful or not. Behavior comes forth from thinking; cubicle or Inspired.

Being Truly Helpful is being present to Inspiration Within, listening and following its guidance.

ACTION: Relax, listen, and open to be Helped. Be humbly available to Inspiration. No hurry. Follow Inspiration as Inspired. No effort, no force, whenever you are willing. The choice is always yours. Inspiration's peace of mind is always ours to choose.

RELAX

Relax now in this moment. Choose relaxation. The best time to relax is now. Awareness of Inspiration Within gives rise to relaxation; a burden is lifted even as you are fulfilling your responsibilities. Do not be afraid to unwind. It can bring the shift you have been working hard at trying to conjure up by yourself. Relax for one moment or more than one moment — relax in this moment.

LISTEN

Listening is a skill acquired by all those who are willing to listen. What does it mean to listen? Listening is being present. Hear the words being spoken to you *and* hear the unspoken.

Silence is beyond the teacher of a 1000 words.

How does one listen to Inspiration Within?
Practice the following now:

- ⊙ Pause your mind. Be still on the inside. Still your body if needed.
- ⊙ Express your willingness to open to Inspiration Within:
   "I am willing."

- ⊙ Allow Awareness to shift to Inspiration's Presence within you.
- ⊙ Rest with a One-Pointed focus on This Presence. Receive.
- ⊙ Listen and Follow This Wisdom revealing itself to you.

STAY AWARE OF BEING CONNECTED

If you become distracted, STAY AWARE OF BEING CONNECTED by:
- ⊙ Notice you are distracted.
- ⊙ Pause.
- ⊙ Return to your willingness to rest in your One-Pointed focus on Inspiration Within.
- ⊙ Listen and Follow.

OPEN TO BE HELPED

Open in your willingness. Open in your willingness not to close. How many ways do you close? There are just as many ways to open. Unclench. Opening to Inspiration's Help is your safety, security and ultimate freedom. Close yourself off and you will experience regret, loneliness, fear and all the angst that fear brings.

Saying yes to the cubicle self is always closing. In closing yourself off in the cubicle mind you will tend to be on guard; offensive or defensive. It is a hard road to tow and yet it is taken again and again and again out of the fear of opening to Love. Sounds crazy. Why would one fear opening to Love? Yet, you do. It is craziness! You fear that which you do not know. Yet, here is the Real Deal. Love knows you and loves you. You do not have to know anything!

In fact, the sooner you admit that you do not know,
The sooner you will see that you do not have to know!
Love knows — and
You are always in Love.

Any moment you can change your mind and whisper "Yes" to Love.

BE HUMBLY AVAILABLE TO INSPIRATION

Being available to Inspiration Within is to humble your false self to This Love. Place your concerns into the hands of Inspiration who will graciously receive them. Take your hands off. Empty your hands. Let go. Humility is the relinquishment of who you think you are or should be, in exchange for who you absolutely are and will always be!

NO HURRY

Slow down. Listening to the voice watching the clock telling you to hurry up? Hmm. Start with slowing down. Even in the midst of body motion the mind can slow down, pause and be still. The body will often follow. Even deciding to slow down your body motion is the decision to stop valuing being in a hurry. It is not that you cannot move at a swift pace and be present to Inspiration Within for certainly

Inspiration is not bound to time as you are. All moments in time are precious to Love for they are time for you to return to Love. Slow down my dear friend.

FOLLOW INSPIRATION AS INSPIRED

Be present. Inspiration will arrive in your awareness. Inspiration may not look as you expect, how you think you want or need or when, but it will arrive. No need to think it all out. Analyzing Inspiration's guidance is postponing or completely avoiding following. Sometimes you do not feel up to following. Follow anyway.

Following is "all in the wrist" so to speak, as you take the hand of this Wisdom Heart and allow your path to be directed. Like a Sunday drive on a Tuesday, be surprised, refreshed and led down a less traveled path — Inspired Way.

NO EFFORT. NO FORCE.

The rope to which you have tethered yourself has been loosened, no longer holding you back. Depend no longer on your own efforts and sheer force. Inspiration walks with you. Sink back now, not in sloth, but in trustful relationship with this Wisdom Within. Stillness washing over any lingering worries about what remains undone. All that needs to be done will be done as needed. Even if for a moment, allow this.

WHENEVER YOU ARE WILLING

Any moment that works for you works for Inspiration Within you. Peace is ready for you whenever you are willing to receive Peace. And if you are not willing, Peace is patient. Such is how Peace is peaceful.

THE CHOICE IS ALWAYS YOURS

You choose. You choose whether or not to follow Inspiration's moment-to-moment calling within you. Let no shame, blame or guilt be laid upon you by your unknowing self for this level of motivation is unworthy of you and an obstacle to receiving true peace. Be present to this Peace and you will naturally be drawn into it. Follow This Peace and see where it leads you — on the inside.

It is natural to now want to extend this Peace that you are receiving in your following. It is a fact that simply by your following Peace in the quiet of your mind, it is being extended. Inspiration may Inspire you to extend this Peace in words, silence, outer action or inner action. Direct guidance will be given on these matters from Wisdom. Wisdom Inspires you to speak, not speak, outer action or inner action. Inspiration never Inspires harm to yourself or another or the world in any way; otherwise it would not be Wisdom to whom you are listening and following. Harm is not The Way.

If you feel strongly to follow in a way that will bring harm, notice you are "feeling to harm" and this is a cue to step back and get out of your own way. Ask Inspiration for help and continue to pause until Peace comes into your awareness. It will come. If need be, the world is full of Inspired helpers — call one. Trust that Inspiration has Wisdom for every situation.

There is violence in this world. How do you face violence? You cannot truly and effectively face the violence appearing outside of you without facing the violence going on inside of you. The choice is one of avoidance or peace. Inner violence is the cause of outer violence. Needless acts of violence occur. How are you to defend yourself? Act wisely, not with hate. Nothing is accomplished through hate. Act without ill will, and great strength and Wisdom will be given you.

Here is where you must face yourself. Evil comes into the world for a purpose — to be overcome by Love. You are unaware of Love's power and so you do not trust it. You think Love is a little thing. Inspiration cannot help the one who thinks so little of Love. You find it easier to trust fear because you have wrestled with it on the outside and know its ways. You have failed to wrestle with Love on the inside and so you do not know Love. Your little knowing knows a "little love."

What does it mean to wrestle with Love? To enter into relationship with This Love — Getting to know This Love. Who is This Love? What is This Love? What does This Love have to do with you, your relationships and your life and the world? Everything. There will come a time in life when you will want to know who you truly are. Love has the answer to that question — it is freely given you. You will not be willing to receive that answer without putting up a fight. Here is the true transformation through Love.

It does not make sense to the common mind as to why anyone would fight against freedom — against recognizing one's True Self. So, what is this wrestling with Love about?

The fear associated with coming into the awareness
Of who you truly are is so great,
That one can barely see to stand it —
The misunderstanding is that when you
Come into the awareness of who you truly are in Love,
It is not that you will not be able to stand —
It is that you will finally be able to see.

The question is this: If a child is having a nightmare, do you lock them inside their room to bear the nightmare alone or do you enter with the strong hand of Love to calm the fear? When you enter with Love a whole battalion enters with Love. When you enter with fear, you enter alone. Which is stronger?

The questions about how, if and when to defend one's self and protect others, and all of life's questions in this world, can draw us to go inside and look to Inspiration Within for our answers. Inspiration Within has the answers. We have to choose to ask the questions, listen and follow. The choice is always ours. Let Inspiration Guide.

INSPIRATION'S PEACE OF MIND IS ALWAYS
OURS TO CHOOSE.

Empty and full all at once — somehow — is This Peace. Personal, yet free to everyone, everywhere is This Peace. All-encompassing without possession. Total Freedom welcomes you. There is nothing you can do to mess it up. No need arises to understand This Peace for in it, all your misunderstanding becomes irrelevant. Welcome Peace.

This Peace is the understanding you have been seeking.

~~~~~~~~~~

WHY PRACTICE PAUSE FOR INSPIRATION, THE 4 DECISIONS?

Practicing Pause For Inspiration, The 4 Decisions is a decision! It is a decision for peace. Peace in your mind, peace in relationships — peace in the world.

WHAT TO EXPECT

Nothing. Expect absolutely nothing. This is very important as this outlook decreases the likelihood of cubicle expectations, based on past experiences and what we think we know, influencing this new moment. The 4 decisions is a present-centered practice Inspired by the Now.

Show up. Come as you are. Extend an invitation to Inspiration Within and say,

"Here I am."

HOW TO BENEFIT EVEN MORE

Consider being willing to commit The 4 Decisions to memory. At the forefront of your mind at all times, you will now have an immediate way for practicing peace, being for — giving and receiving Wisdom.

Committing this practice to memory is a challenge; a challenge that can potentially save you from future cubicle, unnecessary challenges. Even if you are unable to commit the whole practice to memory, there are short phrases varying in length from as little as one word to a few words that will bring you into the Whole Experience, such as: "Rest," "Allow stillness to replace the chatter," "Relax, listen, open to be Helped," "Be humbly available," "Give some space, "I am willing"...

Pause, Step Back, Step Aside and Let Inspiration Guide are easily committed to memory. Adding on each of the decisions is easily accomplished as well:

1. The decision to stop in this moment.
2. The decision to get out of my own way.
3. The decision to invite Inspiration Within to help.
4. The decision to choose my Inspired Mind and follow the Wisdom of Inspiration.

UNDER WHAT CONDITIONS TO PAUSE AND PRACTICE

Practice Pause For Inspiration, The 4 Decisions when you are willing! Willingness is the only condition.

WHEN TO PRACTICE

General Practice Guidelines:

⊙ Practice The 4 Decisions once a day to stabilize awareness of Inspiration Within — this is a suggestion. Mainly, just be willing to use The 4 Decisions when-ever, wherever and with any activity, relationship, situation or circumstance. Do not exclude anything just because you think you already have it under control, it is not important enough or The 4 Decisions does not apply. Inspired Help applies to everything and everyone.

Apply The 4 Decisions to any activity, situation, circumstance and/or relationship before, during and/or after the scene:

⊙ BEFORE: as preparation: calm, efficiency, clarity of focus.

⊙ DURING: to gain greater awareness of Inspiration's presence and direct helpfulness in ordinary life. Be directed as to what and how to communicate, how to accomplish an activity with greater ease, efficiency and creativity, clear communication, patience, being of service to yourself and others.

⊙ AFTER: see yourself and/or another in this moment, notice what you see, what are you learning, what is helpful, what is not helpful, how are you being present to another, to yourself, to Inspiration Within?

These are some examples of how practicing Pausing For Inspiration BEFORE, DURING and AFTER all of our many life events will prove to be helpful. Uncover more and let us know!

Specific Practice While On The Move:

The 4 Decisions is a simple practice to be used eyes open during the activities of everyday life.

⊙ When you are stressed; Before you get stressed; After you have been stressed.

⊙ During a conversation — listening requires pausing within your own mind, thinking, feelings and acting — do not miss out on what is being said — truly respond versus an habitual reaction.

⊙ A person is "not behaving appropriately" — expressing thoughts, words and/or actions — how you think they should.

⊙ During a brief unplanned interaction — even a brief moment can be helpful and meaningful — Inspiration enriches all moments.

⊙ Interactions with children, grandchildren, parents, in-laws, significant other, siblings, companions, friends, co-workers, bosses, employees — all those you communicate with day in and day out.

⊙ Before, During and/or After a party, business dining, social call, networking, engagement with friends and/or family, babysitting, caregiving, disciplining children. You may discover that peace and Inspired thoughts, words and actions show up in the oddest places! Instead of regretting something you did or did not say or do, pause and listen; How are you being Guided?

⊙ Before, During and/or After a business meeting, job interview (interviewer and interviewee), sales call, making an investment decision, routine business calls — why do business as usual when you are being Inspired to do business as Inspired?

⊙ An unexpected phone call, email or "chance" encounter in which someone is asking something of you — money, time, ideas, emotional support — some one needs help and is looking to you. How will you respond?

○ Relationship Help! Whether an intimate relationship with a lifelong partner to a friend, neighbor, family member, acquaintance, or stranger — these all constitute relationships. Ask Inspiration Within how to "be-in" the relationship. Strife and strain can be prevented and a moment of pause experienced instead — for one or both parties.

○ Marketing, advertising, designing, cooking. Inspiration moves you from brainstorming good ideas to true creativity.

○ Get specific guidance in the midst of performing your job — whatever your duties require. Do not ever think that you already know your job and that's that!

○ When making decisions about your heath, fitness, nutrition, sleep, seeing healthcare professionals — go within and listen for what is best for you right now. We can listen to well-meaning people without excluding listening to our Inspired Self.

○ Instead of missing out on an opportunity to Be Truly Helpful at any point in your day — even giving some one an uplifting, reassuring glance — Pause and Practice. Life is a series of moments. It can be a train wreck of fragmentation and disconnection, an off-day or off-interaction that leaves you feeling out of sorts and/or a series of connected, meaningful moments. Connection replaces disconnection.

Specific Practice While Planning

Look ahead by being present first. Moments in the future are very much effected by how you are being present to this moment now.

○ Vacation plans, business plans, plans for teaching a course, planning a family gathering, social get-together, spiritual gathering, where to live, life events, even where to go eat and what to eat... all opportunities to receive Inspiration.

"Quieting"
Pause For Inspiration, The 4 Decisions
as an Extended Practice

Quieting is the practice of using this Guided Practice for at least 4–10 minutes, or longer, while sitting and resting comfortably. Choose one word, one phrase or use the whole practice. No hurry. *Be with.*

You may choose to listen online to the Guided audio practice (go to: www.PauseForInspiration.org) or perhaps record The 4 Decisions in your own voice and listen.

All those new to ideas about centering the mind and living an Inspired Life — a Being Truly Helpful life — will invariably find this practice helpful. At the very least, it will leave you aware of the power of *willingness*. Those who have been centering and living helpful lives for awhile now are being invited to return to the first step, the beginning — the Inspired Heart∞Mind where innocence rests — and this we must do to Be Truly Helpful.

Sharing "The 4 Decisions" Cards
The 4 Decisions Practice on Free 3"x 5" Coated Cards and a Mobile App — Easy to Use; A Joy and Inspiring to Share!

Pause For Inspiration is a nonprofit and one service that we provide is sharing the practice of **"The 4 Decisions"** with people of all walks of life, often one-to-one right on the spot, and to groups of all sizes. The card is going out all over the world! It is a **forgiveness practice at heart with a universal embrace, using language with which anyone could potentially resonate.**

Help With Sharing the Cards and/or Mobile App

I love sharing this practice because it works if I apply it! It is our hope that others will resonate with this universal practice and be Inspired to share it with others. People often share with me how helpful it is to them, but they don't know how to go about sharing it. The way I see it — if you find something that is helpful, share it as Inspired in the moment.

Ways to share the free cards and mobile app:

- ⊙ Pause, Step Back, Step Aside and Inspiration will guide you as to when, where, how and with who to share.
- ⊙ As a clerk gives you your change, give the card in exchange for your change. Say something like, "Oh, here's a card about Pausing For Inspiration." Have fun with it.
- ⊙ Give it to anyone who comes to you for an appointment or to whom you go to for an appointment.
- ⊙ Give it to other "customers" in stores as you find yourself in the casual conversation. So many people are looking for a simple way to de-stress. Everyone is open to a more meaningful life.
- ⊙ People you "run into" anywhere. Remember, there are no accidental meetings. Old friends, new friends, co-workers, ex-bosses, someone from your spiritual community... whoever is right in front of you.
- ⊙ Put it in the envelope with your bill payments.
- ⊙ Include it in greeting cards.
- ⊙ Order a free Inspiration Package on the website and send it as a gift.
- ⊙ Send the card to a friend from the website.

You can share the card at social, spiritual, political, and business gatherings. Let go of what people think of you. Chances are people are not thinking anything about you, but now they can think of you with gratitude for "that card."

- ⊙ Give a stack to business owners, community service organizations, healthcare professionals and whoever will take a stack to share with those they serve!

Sharing fills me with joy as I see the joy in the faces of those receiving. Often when I see someone whom I have given the card to they ask, "Oh, can I have more of those cards!" Immense gratitude I have in these moments for who we truly are, for our willingness to share who we truly are and that in Love all things are possible. Thank you for helping yourself, helping others and helping the world in your being willing to Pause For Inspiration.

TO RECEIVE YOUR FREE CARDS,
INCLUDING FREE SHIPPING
(shipping charge may be applicable outside of U.S.
and Canada) place your order at:

www.PauseForInspiration.org

Pause For Inspiration is a nonprofit 501(c)(3).

Mission:

An Invitation to the
whole world.
Pause For Inspiration
in the midst of everyday life

Pause

Step Back

Step Aside

Let Inspiration Guide

LIVING HEALTH

LIVING HEALTH

TABLE OF CONTENTS

Pause for Inspiration
and Practicing the 4 Decisions
opens the Door to
Experiencing
Living Health

The following material was received directly from

Inspiration Within sharing Wisdom with all of us.

LIVING HEALTH ... and what is it to be alive and well?

LIVING HEALTH IS THE TANGIBLE EXPERIENCE
OF INSPIRATION WITHIN.

INSPIRATION WITHIN is This Boundless Presence of Certain, Constant Love.

To experience This Presence is to Be Truly Helpful for in that moment you have opened and been opened to Inspiration Within. To act in this moment is to Be Truly Helpful for you act with awareness of Certain, Constant Love.

To experience This Presence is to Be Truly Helpful for in that moment you are seeing truly, as you are seeing with Certain, Constant Love.

To act is "to do, to perform an action." To act is also to see others truly. Awareness is action. To Be Truly Helpful is to act—to do and see—from awareness of This Presence. For now you are reminding others who they truly are in Certain, Constant Love—this is the

Inspired Help we can give anyone. It is the Inspired Help we can receive for ourselves. This experience is LIVING HEALTH.

Whether another is in need of food, water, blessing, clothing, a hug, a job, a loving touch, a house, a car or a friend — we are all in need of one very important thing in the midst of our giving to one another — to be "re–minded." To come into awareness of our Inspired Mind experiencing This Love of Inspiration Within, loving us here and now, no matter what; no matter what appearances may hold or words may be saying, you are loved by Love itself.

LIVING HEALTH IS THE TANGIBLE EXPERIENCE OF
KNOWING I AM LOVED.

LIVING HEATH IS THE TANGIBLE EXPERIENCE OF
KNOWING YOU ARE LOVED.

TO KNOW THIS LOVE IS
TO SEE MY INSPIRED AND INSPIRING SELF.

TO KNOW THIS LOVE IS
TO SEE YOUR INSPIRED AND INSPIRING SELF.

LIVING HEALTH IS THE TANGIBLE EXPERIENCE THAT
WE ARE ALL CONNECTED AND IN
TOTAL ABSOLUTE UNION WITH
INSPIRATION WITHIN.

LIVING HEALTH IS FULLY AVAILABLE TO YOU.

What does this all mean?

Tangible Experience is:
Awareness at your core, on the periphery and everywhere
In between; noticeable.

Absolute Union is:
Impossible to separate.

Certain is:
Absolute. Count on it.

Constant is:
Changeless; will never change or go away.

Love is:
Love is the Absolute Definition of Love's Being
Therefore, cannot be defined.
But here goes!
The Complete, Ever Flowing Presence
of All That Is Being
Before the Beginning to Never Ending
to This Now
In You, With You, Through You and Beyond You.
Because of You and the Cause of You.
For You.
Never without.
Never without you.
You are never without.
No one is ever without
All-Encompassing.
No matter what.

Such is how Love is Love,
Flowing in Stillness,
Still Flowing.
Being experienced and shared.

Fully available is:
Already accomplished.
Here, in and with you now.

LIVING HEALTH

BENEFITS

Upon your acceptance of Inspiration Within, you are fully able to experience being in This Certain, Constant, Presence of Love.

LIVING HEALTH IS THE EXPERIENCE OF BEING EFFECTIVE.

We may be effective in making pancakes and playing the stock market and that is all well for breakfast eaters and financial players. LIVING HEALTH speaks of an effectiveness brought forth by the recognition that you are the effect of Inspiration Within; that is, Inspiration Within begins your waking up and your Inspired Self is the effect – it is the awakened one.

DO YOU WANT TO EXPERIENCE BEING EFFECTIVE?

Wake UP!

Most depression is caused by the experience of being ineffective; which precisely means to not know your True Self. One's True Effectiveness is experienced within one's True Self.

WHAT DOES IT MEAN TO BE EFFECTIVE?

Being effective means that you know who you are.

KNOW WHO I AM

Yes, know who you are. This means that you are fully recognizable to your Self. If you have ever looked at yourself in the mirror or caught a fleeting glimpse of yourself in a window, you most likely saw someone you are not. That is, you saw an image of yourself. Who you are, is not that image. Who you are is within. The sooner you get to know who you are the more effective you will be. Until then you will continue to add on or subtract from this image you have of yourself in an attempt to be more effective. You may have an effect in the world and on other people, but this is not to be confused with being truly effective.

LIVING HEALTH EFFECTIVENESS is the experience of being present with your True Self. Step back from this image of yourself and allow Inspiration Within to help you see the real you, if that is what you really want.

BY THE WAY, being effective will make itself known to you in your life in that your time and energy will become tools for your use, rather than time and energy using you up!

LIVING HEALTH IS
A CHARITABLE CONTRIBUTION

Be willing to donate a moment here and a moment there in midst of your day and night, and Inspiration Within will charitably share all the Love you are willing to receive. One morsel of Love carries the full dose.

LIVING HEALTH IS BEING INSPIRED TO BE TRULY HELPFUL.

Your charitable contribution of mere moments here and there results in your being Inspired To Be Truly Helpful to yourself and others. If you want to help yourself and the world, but feel you do not have the time, resources or ideas, begin donating your moments. Everyone has 24/7, resources and ideas; donate some of them to Inspiration Within who will get back with you on how to BEST use them. Don't let your cubicle self eat up all of your time and resources and feed you unprofitable ideas. By the way, time belongs to you. These are your moments to use as you choose. How is your mind using your time?

WHAT DO YOU BELIEVE YOU ARE WORKING AT?

Want the Inside story? Listen, do you hear the sound of your own unfolding? Yes, you! You have an Inside Track — it is you on track with Inspiration Within. Why is this so hard to believe? Because you do not choose to believe. You are busy, so hard working at being busy believing in things that cause you to stumble. Investigate within: what are you believing that is causing you to stumble? What are you not believing? You already know.

Are you believing in things that are no longer sustaining you? Are you believing in a life that is not fulfilling to you. It is not that life is supposed to be a happy party 24/7 — no. In fact, that is one of your distracting beliefs. This human life involves work and challenges; discomfort will arise. The question is: "What are you working at?" Connectedness or disconnectedness?

No need to abandon beliefs that are speaking to you from *Within* and freeing your heart and mind — setting you free to the Inside. Give thanks for these beliefs that are serving yourself and others.

We may believe all kinds of things, the question is, "How are your beliefs helping you and helping others?" Not just "do-gooding" for the sake of cubicle self appearances, but real help. Real help comes from the Inside. You are being drawn to extend love from Within; from the Helper Within who is always standing ready to help you and to help you help another.

LIVNG HEALTH IS THE "HEAL" IN "HEAL-TH"

You need healing. Am I right? You know I am right. This life that you have been planning and worrying about and confiscated, needs healing. While you are going about trying to ignore this fact or trying to heal all the various parts of this life, you may be completely blind to what is in need of healing beneath it all; Not all the parts, but the experience of "being-parted."

Did you notice how as soon as you seem to get one part of your life under control, often another part seems to be laying out there like a dead animal with no hope or a squirrel scrounging for nutrition? This is because your attempting to heal all the various parts is like a circus clown on a trapeze juggling somebody else's business. Healing is the business of Inspiration Within. Let Inspiration do the job.

Inspiration Within knows what needs to be healed: this pervasive sense of being out of sorts, short of change, under the limit, over the limit, cashed out, called in... you name it. You know what I am talking about. It is no accident that the word "health" contains the word "heal."

Bring on your life. What is unhealed? This experience of "being-parted" will show up sooner or later in your relationships, job, daily activities, health, circumstances, situations — in the business of everyday life. So, to address the healing needed in these areas, it is best to address the underlying, pervasive, often unconscious, experience of disconnection in your mind, from Love and from your True Self.

Even as one begins to address "life problems," the irony, is that often what you think is the problem or what appears to be the problem is not the problem at all. Turn towards Inspiration Within, who being aware of the experience of disconnection and dispiritedness, will show you the real problem in your mind. Instead of being distracted by who or what seems to be the problem, Inspiration will give you awareness, sight and help with your life scenario in a way that will allow for healing of the experience of being disconnected — of not experiencing your wholeness.

The good news is that the ultimate answer to all that remains unhealed is the same: recognition, awareness, acceptance and experience of CONNECTEDNESS and UNION in Inspiration Within in whom we are whole, complete and truly loved. Now we are free to love. Watch the problems in your mind fall away as you begin to love. In our being loving, Love heals our experience of "not-Love."

Awareness of being in union with Love brings you back to LIFE. COME IN TO LIFE. Experience Joy in your life.

LIVING HEALTH IS NOT ABOUT APPEARANCES

Living Health is living life from the Inside out. We tend to live life the other way around — from the outside in — that is, from appearances, and then we ingest appearances and wonder why we feel sick or off or disconnected or out of touch. Or perhaps we feel nothing at all. Are you out of touch with the Inside of you? Are you living your life from the outside in or the Inside out?

CAUGHT UP IN APPEARANCES

Where have you been appearing lately? Would you rather be real instead of being an appearance? You have to be willing to connect with this Inside Self. How? Pause For Inspiration. Long pauses, short pauses, daytime pauses, nighttime pauses, still pauses, moving pauses, body pauses — PAUSE already! LIVING HEALTH is the willingness to check-in.

LIVING HEALTH IS
EXPERIENCING YOUR VALUE

You are not valuable of your own accord, your own choices, your own doing, your own makings, your own accomplishments — "OUCH, THAT HURTS," screams the cubicle self. You are valuable because you are the recipient of something of great value — LIFE.

Reminder: Your human life is valuable, and yet if you were to open up to LIFE, this Loving Certainty within you, how much more valuable your human life would prove to be.

LIVING HEALTH IS A CHANGE OF MIND

What does this mean, "being transformed?" We hear this word "transformation" thrown around a lot: transform your relationship, your marriage, your body, your kitchen! Hmm. To be transformed is to be in the presence of Love. Love is new every moment we touch it. I cannot speak for your kitchen, but this is sure – your life will be transformed and transforming to others as you rest in the presence of Love. Any given moment will do; you do not have to wait for some future moment or special event. Love IS the "NOW" you may have been hearing about.

*It is impossible to not be loving in the awareness of
the presence of Love — impossible!*

LIVNG HEALTH IS TRUSTING THAT THERE IS AN INSPIRED PLAN FOR YOUR LIFE. WHICH LIFE WOULD THAT BE?

Yeah, yeah, I know you've heard this before. What plan? The plan you are not making, tracking and predicting; that's what plan. Listen, you have a limited amount of time here on this earth. Do you really want to spend it devising a plan that is all about you and your "best" interests? How is it going? Maybe it is going well, maybe not. "I have a plan for you," rings the voice of Certainty.

Is Inspiration's plan all peaches and pools of fresh water? No. It is so much more than that. This plan is nothing that you can imagine and yet everything that is already yours upon your acceptance.

You often think about how to live your life, but you get only so far in this life because you have forgotten "LIFE." LIFE is the gift. LIFE itself is the plan, the gift for you. Do you see? Life has been given you. Not solely your human being "life;" I speak of LIFE. It is that which you are seeking that cannot be planned by you for it has already been planned for you, with you and given you. This is the aliveness you are seeking. It is Within.

LIFE IS CURRENTLY IN SESSION.
ARE YOU IN OR OUT?

LIVNG HEALTH IS TO BE EXPERIENCED

Oh, are we going to get all touchy feely now? I am teaching you about inner experience. Inspiration Within wants you to experience Inspiration for yourself. Thus, you were given an Inspired Mind. Experiences are highly overrated and misunderstood. They are overrated by those who do not know the truth about Love, for if they did, they would not be chasing after fleeting feel good experiences — emotional highs always followed by emotional lows always followed by seeking more highs. Experiences are misunderstood in this chase. They are seen as the end all and be all — the culmination of some cubicle quest.

LIVING HEALTH is an experience that fully benefits you and others as it is an experience given you by Inspiration Within. You cannot make these experiences up as the cubicle self is prone to trying to do; always falling short of the real thing.

Remember this LIFE we were talking about? I am going to keep bringing this up because it is so important and you keep forgetting about LIFE as you focus on "making a life for yourself." Chill out. No one is going to take away your life that you made. This is not a divorce settlement! THIS LIFE is CONTINUALLY experiencing LOVE. A True Experience, one *given* by Inspiration Within, calls Love out into the world. It literally extends Love into the world. Speak it aloud or not, but you cannot keep it to yourself for your own little personal experience collection — when you notice Love, Love puts everyone on notice. Love is a True Experience. A True Experience always bears itself out — in you, through you and into others whether they are aware of it or not.

Each public hearing that you attend will give you more Love; Love that you can then use to be Inspired To Be Truly Helpful.

LIVING HEALTH IS NOT AIRY FAIRY

Let's talk about airy fairy. Airy fairy is you placing faith in your cubicle self. For this cubicle self is full of hot air and lost in the world's fair!

LIVING HEALTH IS
AN INNER EXPERIENCE

Not an idea, a concept or an intellectual game. LIVING HEALTH is an experience of a very Real, Infinite Love abiding in you. And in your inner experience of This Real Love, it is now possible for you to give This Love. Mental construction zones put up walls; LIVING HEALTH is watching the walls fade away. You have put up some interior walls that are not on the BLUEPRINT. Hence, the floor plan is not working and you are walking on substitute ground. Huh?

LIFE (remember) provides us with Infinite Space to roam free. When selfishness set in, we each wanted our own space so we put up walls. We became selfish because we felt unsafe. We felt unsafe because we chose to think without Inspiration Within, without Love. These walls are affecting your experience of who you think you are — this cubicle false self. You believe this false self is your personhood.

Let me tell you of your REAL personhood – the person who is living from This LIFE we have been speaking of. This is your true person-hood. Thus, LIVING HEALTH is highly inner personal, but not how you generally think of "personal." The cubicle self takes its person-ality and feelings and thoughts and behaviors very personally, and that of others. What about this? Do you really believe that you are nothing more than the sum total of all this? No wonder you are bored and distracted! YOU ARE MORE THAN THIS. Yes, you are having a human experience. LIVING HEALTH is opening to the experience of the Real You, the Inspired You.

A HEALING PRACTICE

In these now moments allow yourself to open to experiencing who you are, who another is and who we are together.

~ rest ~

LIVING HEALTH becomes a tangible experience for _(your name)_ , as I recognize my connection to This Certain, Constant Love in the core of my being.

~ rest ~

LIVING HEALTH is shared with _(another's name)_ , as I recognize that he/she is connected to This Certain, Constant Love in the core of his/her being.

~ rest ~

LIVING HEALTH becomes a tangible experience for _(your name)_ , as I recognize that I am one spark of This Certain, Constant Love. This one spark is my Inspired Self.

~ rest ~

LIVING HEALTH is shared with _(this person's name again)_ , as I recognize that he/she is one spark of This Certain, Constant Love. This one spark is his/her Inspired Self.

~ rest ~

LIVING HEALTH is the recognition that you and I, and all, are connected, spark to spark, within This Certain, Constant Love.

~ rest ~

LIVING HEALTH is the recognition that all of the "one sparks" shine forever forth from the Totality that is Life.

~ rest ~

LIVING HEALTH
ESTABLISHES YOUR INDIVIDUALITY

No fear need be had over losing your individuality — that which is you and is your gift to the world. As we choose Love, these interior false ceilings, floors and walls begin to fade. Does this mean we are all falling into one another and losing our individual identity? No. In fact, you will grow towards and into your true identity as you move in Love's direction — this is what freedom allows. One's true identity is sure of Itself, for it is identified from Within. Now, you are free to experience LOVE in the world.

LIVING HEALTH IS THE SPIRIT OF YOU

Inspiration is not only an idea; it is a reality of the highest degree that one can encounter here through our human experience. It communicates through your spirit. YOU HAVE A SPIRIT. How about that? Now, commerce and some mislabeled "spiritual" systems have futzed around with the word "spirit" and led many into a conundrum. If you are led into confusion by anyone referring to "spirit," he is not coming from True Spirit but from his own effort. Though we hear about the "spirit" of things from cars to diapers, Spirit, and your spirit, thankfully do not fall (and I mean fall) into these misunderstandings.

LIVING HEALTH IS
FULLY APPLICABLE IN COMMERCE

Business cannot be held apart from Inspiration Within. Well, it can, but look at the result. Cubicle "partnerships" "takeovers" "liquidations" "bail-outs" etc. Sounds like a bad night at sea. Tummy upset? Do business differently. How? With your Inspired Self. Imagine being a seller of goods and services and sharing Inspiration. Customers want to be Inspired; any good business person knows the power of Inspiration. Unknowing business people try to use seduction, persuasion and even temptation instead of Inspiration. "Buy this car from me and I'll take you for a ride." This kind of transaction is using a customer and misusing one's self. The result is a customer feeling used and not returning to close the deal or make another purchase. The business person also winds up feeling used. A user will eventually feel used because he has misused his mind.

The cubicle mind can get all fired up in anger or in excitement. The Inspired Mind is a willing camper around the campfire of Inspiration Within; being a spark of Inspired creativity amidst stale tactics, protocols and procedures. Sharing Inspiration one-to-one. In Inspiration's presence the cubicle mind with its worn out cubicle approaches is relieved of its toil, so now work that is useful, productive and abundant comes forth. The Inspired Mind is invigorated and invigorates. The Inspired Mind shines a light on how to be Inspired To Be Truly Helpful. Let's warm up the world.

Be the light in the darkness. Be the fire of joy in your work place instead of waiting for someone else to crack a smile. Be the one who is willing to see anew — notice the good job of your coworker — not waiting around for someone to take note of your work. Be the one doing your job to the tune of Inspiration instead of simply admiring a colleague who is stepping to the rhythm of Inspiration. Be the one who is Inspired to Inspire others instead of waiting for someone else to Inspire you. Be the one who sees a customer as an opportunity to experience what your Inspired Mind is up to, instead of seeing the customer as simply a means to a paycheck or an annoying gnat to swat!

It begins with you. Do not use your company policies or your boss or your co-workers or the economy to make excuses for you not being the light, not being helpful. You are the light! Go and be a light at sea. Take out your lifeboat and go shopping for customers drowning in dispiritedness — go fishing for colleagues who have forgotten who they truly are outside of the cubicle mind. Those lost at sea will look to you. Now who is the boss? Inspiration is not looking to keep people in their place like ducks in a row quacking out the singsong of the cubicle mind. Inspiration sees you and sees a swan of great delight floating in an ocean of Grace. Pause, Step Back, Step Aside and Let Inspiration Guide. Be the swan!

It is not about appearances. You do not have to take over or cause a raucous coup. Mind the change Inspiration is ready to bring about on the inside of you. Be led from Within how to be Inspired in commerce. Don't be surprised if others see you as foolish. Be prepared for True Wisdom. Be wise and profit.

LIVING HEALTH IS PROFITABLE

ALERT, DISCLAIMER: The following is not a solicitation for donations to WNYHOO–NOW, Inc. (World Needs Your Help One-to-One—NOW! dba Pause For Inspiration)!

Money is one aspect of being profitable. If you have a lot of money, it is wise to give a portion away as Inspired from within. If you have very little money, it is wise to give some of it away. This is because you do not appreciate the value of the money you have until you let some of it go. One must appreciate the value of money before becoming willing to let Inspiration Within teach you how to use your money. Give some away, then you will know the true value of your money.

Hold on, don't get your George Washingtons all feathered up. Listen, a responsibility has been brought upon you if you have money. It is your responsibility to use it wisely. Your Inspired Self offers you Wisdom that you will then apply to life, including matters of the dollar. For it is not just the spending of a dollar, but hate or love being released into the world. As you spend money, from what motivation and place within you are you spending the money? Is it from Wisdom, habit, longing, being discontent and/ or dissatisfaction? In other words, is your manner of spending money, investing money, saving money coming forth from fear and disconnection or connection?

Money is a high priced item in this life. So, the question is, "Can you afford to not question how you handle money?" You may go ahead and keep it all inside a safe for yourself alone, but it isn't doing all the good it could be doing you there! If you want your money to work for you, let Inspiration Within work for your money. Here is the deal: If you are not allowing Inspiration Within to teach you how to use your money, you don't have any money; your money has you. It does not belong to you anyway. It is in your safe, keeping, or it is placed in the hands of Inspiration, who has the money and your "best interest" in mind.

LIVING HEALTH IS FREE

What? Healthcare is not free and it sure is not cheap. Well, looky here, free healthcare. Inspiration Within cares about your health. Yes, I know you have arteries and so forth and so on. Do you really believe that your health is solely about your arteries? Please, eat right and take care of your arteries and all bodily involvements. I want you to stick around until you get this LIVING HEALTH thing, then you are free to go. Just do not go before you have accepted LIVING HEALTH.

You may have all your health categories in line, OR NOT: eyesight, hearing, cholesterol, blood pressure, bone density, strength, endurance... but do you have your mind in line? In line with your Inspired Self that is? When you hear "LIVING HEALTH" the body may come to mind. One's body is not the whole package mind you. You can be full of health as measured up by the world, yet have no Living Health. You can be lacking in health as measured by the world, yet be full of Living Health.

LIVING HEALTH IS ON THE INSIDE

Living Health is the health that is already Inside of you. IT CAME FREE WITH THAT "LIFE" we were talking about. You are wondering, "Well, if it came free, how come I didn't know about it before now?" You did know. You forgot. And you listened to the advice of a lot of other people who also forgot. Here is your reminder. Listen to the LIFE that is in you.

LIVING HEALTH IS BEING A LEADER

Your Inspired Self is a natural leader. This is because it is focused on the Inspired Self in others. Your Inspired Self is simply leading others into their Inspired Self. All will be thankful for this. Who will you lead to see their Inspired Self today?

LIVING HEALTH IS BEING A FOLLOWER

To follow is not to mimic. Follow Love and you will come to your fruition. It takes humility to follow, not stupidity; strength, not weakness. Humility is highly intelligent for it recognizes that there is a possibility that is more outstanding than what appears at first glance. The Inspired Self leads well because it follows WELL — it follows Inspiration Within. Follow with a one-pointed focus on the Inside Track. A poor leader looks about to see what everyone in the cubicle wants — the cubicle does not know what it wants. This leader now becomes a follower of cubicle confusion. Now, a lost leader leads. Following Inspiration Within is a lessening of one's false self and a growing into one's True Self. A true leader looks Within and leads you there — to the Within in you. As you follow Inspiration Within, you are leading. Who are you following?

LIVING HEALTH IS NOT A BOXING MATCH

You can take your gloves off because there are not two of you in the ring; a cubicle self in one corner and an Inspired Self in the opposite corner fighting it out. No one is standing over some poor "soul" lying on the ring floor giving him ten seconds to get up or go down in defeat. No referee is shaking the arm of the winner in the air declaring him the reigning champ. In LIVING HEALTH no one loses. The cubicle self is its own punching bag; sound familiar? Like a mad dog it just keeps coming back for more, dazed and confused. Oh, it may have on shiny new trunks and be smiling ear to ear, but it is still dazed and confused. The cubicle self is a glutton for punishment; self-punishment. Your Inspired Self is seated comfortably in the front row and is clearly aware of the cubicle self boxing with itself in its boxed up world. Your Inspired Self sees and throws one thing into the ring that changes the whole scene — Love. The cubicle self does not lose so much as it is gradually released from its' duties as you are willing to be released into Love. So, take off your boxing gloves, give up your cubicle corner in the ring and step out of the cornered cubicle self. You are a perfect match for your Inspired Self.

LIVING HEALTH DOES NOT PIT DARKNESS AGAINST LIGHT

These human times can feel pretty dark and pretty lonely and it is not pretty. What good is the light when you are in the darkness and cannot see the light? The light sees you; this is all you need remember. Even in what seems to be the greatest darkness, there is an even greater light. Even when you cannot see, hear, touch, taste, smell or feel the presence of this light, it is *with* you. This Light is here because you are here and it is on the Inside of you — remember? Want to know how to remember? Help someone else. LIVING HEALTH is the light in the darkness — be the light for that is what you are. Be the light right where you are.

When you are in the dark, remember, you are not out of the Light. This Light illuminates all of your darkness and is unlimited in its illumination.

LIVING HEALTH IS FOR-GIVING

"For-Giving." That means to be "for" giving. What does it mean to be "for?" And what is it that you are "giving?" To be "for" is to be an instrument of whom is for you — Inspiration Within is for you, not against you. And it is in you and through you that Inspiration Within extends this "being for" to others. For you to "be-for" is to be willing to allow Inspiration Within to give of Itself — Love — to others, through you. Love is what you are giving to others as it is Love that Inspiration Within is always giving to you.

Unwrap forgiveness in whatever it is you have been wrapping it up in and saving for another day. You may not have another day. The one whom is in need of your for-giving may not have another day. What are you wrapping un-for-giving in? Could it be that you believe you are not the recipient of having been forgiven? That is often the case you know. Yes, you know — your Inspired Self knows anyway. It is this erroneous belief that keeps you from for-giving. You do not realize that you have for-giving to give because you do not realize it has been *given* you. ASK FOR WHAT YOU DO NOT REALIZE SO THAT YOU MAY REALIZE IT.

Or maybe you erroneously believe that you are not in need of forgiveness. Listen, your Inspired Self is in no need for it knows who it is. But there is this needy little cubicle self character gnawing at you at all times of the day and night with confusion, doubt, striving, not being good enough, not being successful, vengeance, perfectionism, jealously, arrogance, guilt, shame, on and on. This guy needs some for-giving! Please! Help this guy! How? Recognize the cubicle condition and open to a change of mind. Give it into Inspiration Within in whom all darkness falls away.

In noticing what appears to be another's cubicle self, be the light in the darkness. Come forth as an instrument of Inspiration Within, willing to see this one beyond who he or she appears to be in this moment — be willing to see his or her Inspired Spark. In your willingness, give over your cubicle self and see beyond the appearance of another's cubicle self; open to healing for the both of you. You are Being Truly Helpful. You will be guided exactly how to go about being an instrument of Inspiration Within as the moment arises. Pause. It will become clear how to see as you allow.

True forgiveness is the recognition and acceptance that you have been *given* something of great value — your Inspired Self — and are now offering this Greatest Gift to another. Listen, others do not know about your Greatest Gift and you do not either until you give it. They do not know about their Greatest Gift, but are waiting for someone to show them that they too have an Inspired Self. So, for-giving is not about letting some poor schmuck off the hook for something. For-giving is about withdrawing the hook this "schmuck" has in you and you have in this "schmuck." True for-giving is seeing beyond the schmuck's errors to the presence of Inspiration Within. Otherwise it sounds like one-schmuck, two schmuck. For-give already. Go ahead, get on with it.

How come you withhold for-giving like it is a precious commodity? You are afraid that if you for-give this schmuck, this includes yourself as well, he is going to get away with this nonsense! Unfair labor tactics! Furthermore, you will be the schmuck letting him get away with this nonsense! The gossip is that no one is allowed to be set free from her nonsense and this "no one" needs to be forever held accountable for her nonsense. After all, others are still holding you accountable for your nonsense! Herein lies the decision to not for-give.

Focusing solely on one's error and not seeing beyond the error holds everyone hostage to the inevitable errors of the cubicle mind. You are all falling into error on a regular basis and hold yourself and others in error in your unwillingness to for-give. You may say you "for-give" one's actions, yet still hold this one prisoner to the cubicle self that made the error. Remember, the cubicle self condition is to be caught up in making mistakes, errors in judgment. This is all the cubicle self "knows" for it does not know Inspiration Within. No true for-giving can happen in the cubicle mind, for to truly for-give is to see this one beyond the error. If you make a mistake, do you want it to be held against you eternally? Now who is caught up in nonsense?

It is not that someone will not have to face in the world the worldly consequences for one's cubicle errors and tragic acts. Such is the world's way of dealing.

Not for-giving is painful, painful, painful, painful. Not for-giving breeds pain and suffering. Not for-giving is not for you. WITHOUT BEING FOR-GIVING YOU WILL NOT KNOW THAT YOU HAVE BEEN FORGIVEN. No matter how you size it up — you will not receive awareness of the fact that you are forgiven. Without for-giving there will be no LIVING HEALTH.

True for-giving is giving that which has been *given* you — being seen truly, beyond the cubicle condition. Beyond this world's way of forgiving. True for-giving is seeing beyond error, beyond appearances, beyond the verdict of guilt and shame. True for-giving is accepting healing by recognizing that there is no error so great that our Inspired connectedness to one another can ever be severed. Bodies may be separated. There may be separations in relationships and partnerships. But your Inspired Self and another's Inspired Self can in no way ever be separated. This is the true nature of the Inspired Self who has not been condemned, therefore does not condemn. This is an Inspired fact that the cubicle self in its cubicle condition cannot begin to understand, accept or see. This is exactly why we need the Inspired Self; precisely why we cannot practice true for-giving without the Help of Inspiration Within.

NOTE: For-giving will only operate in cooperation with Inspiration Within. Attempting for-giving without Inspiration Within will cause the for-giving tool to malfunction. For best results apply for-giving with Inspiration Within. See your Inspired Self for specific instructions.

Accept that you have been truly for-given so now you may truly for-give.

LIVNG HEALTH BRIDGES THE GAP BETWEEN THE TWO MINDS

LIVING HEALTH bridges the experience of having two minds. You do not actually have two minds, but you are double-minded. You vacillate between false and true; this is the double-mindedness that leads to doubt. "False" simply means disconnectedness from Inspiration Within and "True" is the fact of being joined with Inspiration Within. How does LIVING HEALTH bridge this gap? By offering you the clear choice between the two. You need not be confounded any longer. You are free to choose either way of perceiving, but know that if you are confused, doubtful and afraid, you have simply chosen the mind believing in disconnection. Thankfully, believing in disconnection does not make it true. It is however, the cause of all dispiritedness. Thus, Inspiration Within your Inspiring Heart∞Mind is the covered Bridge that takes us over the gap between perceiving disconnection to perceiving union. Without Inspiration Within, your attempts to bridge this gap all by your me-some self will result in falling into the gap again and again which frankly is not a wise approach. After enough pain, heartache and suffering you will eventually, pause, before leaping into the gap without a Safety Net. Such is Wisdom.

LIVING HEALTH IS "BEING PRESENT"

Okay, you may have been hearing about the importance of "being present." Does anyone know what that means? Shall I take out my stopwatch and start timing my being present? Shall I set a goal to be present for the next 10 seconds, 5 minutes, 20 minutes, 1 hour, all day? Do I need to sit down to be present or can I stand up? Do I have to stop talking to be present? Do I have to tell somebody else to shut up so I can be present? Do I have to find a special place to be present? Does the body have to be in a special position to be present? What is the deal anyway? Does anybody know how to "be present?"

Yes. The answer to your question is, "Yes." Your Inspired Self knows and is fully present. Pausing to experiencing your Inspired Self is a way to be present. Simply pause and invite Inspiration Within into your awareness. Now, rest. Go ahead, right now, pause, close your eyes if need be though this is not necessary (especially if you are driving or operating any machinery!) and invite Inspiration Within into your awareness. Really, take a few moments right here and practice being willing to be present. I will pause now and join with you.

. . . .*Pausing* . . . .

What a relief. What a relief to pause. Pause instead of judge. Pause instead of talk. Pause instead of analyze. The greatest obstacle to pausing is judging. Judging is to place my cubicle beliefs, perceptions and experiences upon another and compare them to what I perceive are that person's cubicle beliefs, perceptions and experiences. Judging is full participation in a cubicle affair. We all have a love affair with judgment because we are having a love affair with our cubicle self. The cubicle self walks a tightrope of judgments, falling with each one and paying a great cost: the ongoing experience of dispiritedness.

Mixed up in this cubicle affair is analyzing. Analyzing has its place in problem solving or achieving clarity, but more often than not analyzing is used in place of Inspiration Within. All of the analysis in the world will not return you to the awareness of your forgiven self; Intellectual thinking about this forgiven self will not bring you into true, lasting awareness. Analysis cannot and will not fulfill your one and only need — to be loved.

Why do we all have a need to be loved? Precisely because we are unaware of the fact that we are loved. But you will not know this until you are willing to be present, to rest in Love. Pause.

Being present is the action required to take an action in the world that changes the world; changes the world because it changes you — and changes the person to whom you are being present.

Pausing is the "ultimate action" if you will, because it allows for the Ultimate Love to act instead of me, yet through the true me who knows it is loved. Now, I am being present.

LIVING HEALTH IS CATCHING ME BEFORE, DURING AND AFTER I FALL...AGAIN

We are each falling away from being present to Inspiration Within in any given moment. It seems we ascend into Love only to descend as if further away from where we started — wherever that is. No matter how close to Love we think we are, Love is always closer than we think — and closer than our thinking. No matter how far away from Love we feel we have fallen, Love has taken the fall with us. It cannot be of our own efforts that we walk this path of LIVING HEALTH, for it is not a solo trip. Guess what? There is a reason we are all here: to catch one another! Is that an Inspired Plan or what? I am here to catch you. You are here to catch me — Inspiration Within being the Net, of course.

So if you see someone falling into judgment, gossip, analysis, despair — disconnectedness. What do you do? What is your part? Do you just sit there and go "Whoa, there they go. Yeah, there goes another one?" Yes and no. That is, sometimes you say something and sometimes you don't; sometimes you do something and sometimes you don't. Be Inspired. But whether you say or do anything or not, pause within and ask for help from your Inspired Self. Direction will be given from your Inner Teacher as to how to proceed from here that may or may not involve words and/or physical actions. Listen. Pausing and listening is an action within itself.

This is important:

Inner Guidance may not involve words or actions in catching another's fall. You may be guided from Within to simply practice for-giving. How do I practice for-giving? How do I catch another before, during or after a fall into one's cubicle mind?

Here is Both a Catching and Fall Prevention Plan

Pause, Step Back, Step Aside and Let Inspiration Guide.

It works (if you put it into practice).

This will invariably require being willing to exchange

Your old habitual ways of reacting and communicating.

This is a job only to be filled by your Inspired Heart∞Mind.

Don't wait for the next canned good drive or charity event or when you are closer to "enlightenment"— help the falling now. Those around you, in your very midst, are falling into their cubicle minds and need to be caught before the next, perhaps even greater fall. For when I catch another, I too am caught. Just remember that your cubicle self is not the one doing the catching. Pause, Step Back, Step Aside and Let Inspiration Guide — Love is a Sure Catch.

LIVING HEALTH IS TAKING ACTION

LIVING HEALTH is both inner action and outer action. Inner action is willingness. Willingness may appear passive, but in fact it is an action of great proportion. Inner action includes the willingness to pause and survey your false self with Inspiration

Within — you have to know what you have been drawn into before you can let it go; otherwise, you will continue to be drawn into it.

Outer action is stepping out into the world from the Inside. Your outer action, when coming forth from the Inside Track, will prove to be of much greater value than outer action taken from the false self. However, if Love is what you are after, you will find Love. Allow your True Self to act in the world. Hearts and minds are waiting on you to take action: inner and outer.

LIVING HEALTH IS
LETTING "ME" GO

This "me" most everyone believes themselves to be has shown up here already and is showing up here again because it is of utmost importance to opening to see that you are so much more than "me!" This can be a hard pill to swallow. Get yourself a glass of water. Here goes. How are you seeing yourself? Do you only see a "me?" After years of struggling to advance and enhance this "me-character" I am happy to tell you that LIVING HEALTH is not about this "me." You are not this "me" you have been believing yourself to be. The hardest part of practicing LIVING HEALTH is giving up me. All problems, judgment and despair are based in the belief that "I am me." This sounds silly, but, no, you are not this "me."

To believe you are this cubicle me has left you stranded in the sea of me. Who are you if you are not me? You are YOU – the True You. The longer you hold onto this me the more pain and suffering you are going to experience; this is because me is alone, even in relationships me is alone. The longer you cling to the sea of me, your life support, LIVING HEALTH, is being held at bay.

One morning I awoke and saw how my life is not about me! What an eye opener. I am eternally grateful. What a relief! It's not about me!

WHAT IS LIFE ABOUT?

So, if this life is not about me, who is it about? Love. True purpose will not be found in me because me will never love. Do you need to get another glass of water? It is not the job of me to undo me or get rid of me. Me will be let go of in my willingness to let Inspiration Within loosen my grip on me.

One will never find one's truth in this me because me will never know real love. LIVING HEALTH is living love. Not the "love" we usually think of as love. Real Love. Real Love comes from Inspiration Within not from this me I believe myself to be. LIVING HEALTH is not trying to figure out how Love loves. LIVING HEALTH is allowing LOVE to love.

HOW DOES THIS LOVE LOVE?

Through you! We hear talk about how the world needs more loving people. What are we all waiting for? Some special people to show up who are specially equipped to love? You are the loving people. You have been *given* a Loving Self. This Self is your constant companion amidst the comings and goings of daily living through which Inspiration Within enters your life in a very practical, useful way. Be willing to see that as you are making decisions, moving through your daily routine and engaging in your relationships, this Inspired Self is right there with you. It is whispering in your ear, "Here I am." It is laughing, skipping, jumping, riding along with you in the car, there with you while you are watching shows and movies, reading a book, exercising, shopping, caregiving, raising children ... not judging you, but reminding you who you are.

LIVING HEALTH is your awareness of the presence of peace. LIVING HEALTH is being aware that you are literally connected to this Steady Stream of Peace who is seeing a much bigger picture of life than the cubicle mind is seeing. Beyond that, LIVING HEALTH is being willing to let This Peace give you guidance, help, ideas, strength, energy, clarity, mental focus, ways of moving one's body, true creativity, patience, on and on... Your Inspired Self is not a concept; it is real!

TO BE TRANSFORMED

Pause and open. Being present to Presence. Ask This Love, "Who are you?" Ask, "Who am I?' You will experience an answer. Misunderstanding still abounds in the belief that no such thing as Loving Presence exists or that it may exist, but have nothing to do with our everyday lives. Another misconception is that the Inspired Self is the cubicle self on a good day. No. Your cubicle self will never become an Inspired Self — ever! And yet, it will fall away in Love's presence. Your Inspired Self is present with you here on earth and can be of great use. It is moving through you, with you and in you.

I GOTTA DO WHAT?

Okay, now that you are resonating with your Inspired Self, or at least contemplating the possibility, LIVING HEALTH is also being aware of your connection to other people's Inspired Self! How's that for a bargain? What is this for? No worries. This is not an extra assignment. As you are aware of the presence of your Inspired Self, you cannot help but be aware of this invisible thread to another's Inspired Self, an intricate web of connection among us all. In fact, it is often easier to notice this Inspired Self first in another before you notice it is also in you.

LIVING HEALTH IS BEING HELD FREE

Grace is something that is hard to put into words for it is beyond anything words in the world have to offer. Grace is an experience of being free on the Inside; Something is holding you and yet, you are being held without restraint. You want to be held, you do not mind being held — for somehow in being held you are free.

This "being held free" holds out no hoops for you to jump through. Grace is offered. Offered for your acceptance. Acceptance of Grace brings immense freedom. It is the Catcher and the Net even when it seems there is no Catcher and no Net. So, in your cubicle self you will fall from Grace, but Grace has not fallen away from you. Such is Grace. The offer stands.

LIVING HEALTH IS HELPING THE WORLD

The world is not going to go away through my ignorance, denial, inattention, wishful thinking or plopping it in someone else's lap. The world is not a separate entity; it is you and all of the rest of us. Thus, when I help the world, I help myself and when I help myself, I help the world.

WORLD NEEDS YOUR HELP
ONE-TO-ONE — NOW!

There is something we all want in this life and though we may not be able to describe it or name it exactly, I will venture to give it a descriptive name, "simple, uncomplicated love." Here we are, all of us, making up this world. That's right, we are the world. Last I checked, this world, that would be all of us, needed some help. What kind of help? Simple, uncomplicated love.

Inspiration is asking for volunteers. The cubicle self is volunteering dispiritedness and selling dispiritedness, often at a hefty price. Your Inspired Self is volunteering to be Inspiring and that is free. The choice is mine. Which will I volunteer in this moment? What I choose, I get. What I get, the world gets.

LIVING HEALTH IS THE RECOGNITION THAT THERE IS A CENTER AND IT IS NOT ME!

In this "me" driven society the sadly mistaken are sad precisely because the grave error that they have made is that they are the Center — the Center around which everything and everyone else revolves. Upon first glance, none of us would say that we experience ourselves as the Center, but we do, upon second glance. Being the Center of my own little universe is the natural habitat of the cubicle mind; a place it calls "home."

Until one is willing to relinquish this self-centered approach to managing and operating one's life, one distances oneself from LIVING HEALTH. This is hard for the cubicle self to swallow because being its own center is the only life it knows. Yet, remember LIFE? Yes, you have another LIFE and this LIFE is fully available to you here in this human life. But you will not be aware of this LIFE until you relinquish the position of "full-time head honcho" in your human life.

When you are ready to open to this LOVE, this LOVE that is not a "love" of your own making that waxes and wanes, but a LOVE that is a CONSTANT CENTER, will arrive into your awareness. In this inner awareness LIFE will pour itself out upon you and reach out from Indwelling, again, as it did in the beginning, and in this, everything will fall into place if only for a moment's glimpse. Everything will fall into place in that the true meaning of you, your life, your relationships, this world and your purpose in it will be revealed. This revelation will take place because you will have welcomed it, having set aside this "me" if only for a moment or perhaps it occurs not because of anything we say or do, but is all Grace. In this experience of this CONSTANT CENTER you will see that you too are a part of it.

LIVNG HEALTH IS THE WHOLE CAKE ~~~~~~~

Okay, this is going to really upset the cubicle mindset. Thus far the cubicle self has been getting away with taking a dab or two here and there of that which is Inspired and mixing it in with its own brand of "Inspiration" which is not Inspired. Cubicle brand Inspiration is easy to spot; it sounds too good to be true — that is because it is not true! Not that true Inspiration does not sound good, for it absolutely does and IS; however, what makes true Inspiration sound good, but perhaps seems a bit of a challenge, as compared to cubicle so-called "Inspiration," is that your cubicle self cannot participate. In cubicle brand Inspiration, that cubicle self is a wound up party doll making its way through the room being the good host, appearing to be "Inspiring."

What am I talking about? Example: there is something in your life, in everyone's life, that they have been striving to have be a certain way — the way they think it should be. This could be a husband, wife, partner, a job, a child, a parent, a friend, a project, a career, a hobby, a business, a body etc. Occasionally, you experience a moment of Inspiration around the subject at hand or you read a book or talk to someone and experience how this situation or relationship or whatever, could truly be Inspired. All excited about the Inspiration you decide to apply it to your scenario that you are trying to improve, uplift, or shape up. It does help and you see the benefit, but then before long Inspiration doesn't seem to be helping. You have somehow retreated and nothing has truly changed. In fact, in a relationship, conflict can reach an all time high; a business may take a down turn; a career may get hijacked when you lose your job; you are diagnosed with an illness or get injured or gain a few pounds. What happened? You applied Inspiration and things were better for a short time, but then everything took a dive. Who needs this kind of Inspiration?

The trip to LIVING HEALTH will almost always involve conflict at some level. Why? Often, not always, but often, this is due to trying to fit Inspiration into the cubicle; it is like trying to bottle sunshine. The cubicle self is seeking help, but then when Inspired Help is given, it wants to somehow keep its current scenario and add a touch of Inspiration to it so that the current scenario will improve, but only how the cubicle self thinks it should improve. The cubicle self seeks change, but only to a certain extent; it doesn't want there to be so much change that it becomes obsolete!

You see, the cubicle self is trying to decorate its cake with Inspiration, but it is still the same cubicle cake!

Meanwhile, Inspiration is offering a whole new recipe, from scratch!

LIVING HEALTH IS SHIFTING INTO AN INSPIRED PARADIGM

Most of us are open to the idea of saying yes to Inspiration's help, but only to a certain point. We say "Yes, welcome," until we start feeling uncomfortable, then we say, "Thanks for dropping in, BYE." That's okay, for we naturally tend to take baby steps out of the cubicle self and often take giant leaps right back into the cubicle self even as we are moving out of it. It happens. Not that Inspiration causes discomfort. No, for it is the Comforter. It is the cubicle self that is uncomfortable as it squirms its way around looking for a spot to call home and not in the neighborhood of Inspiration. Inspiration is welcome to hang out on the edges of the cubicle subdivision, dressing up the landscaping perhaps, but no way will the cubicle self allow Inspiration to move in next door.

One common problem in the cubicle is romantic/significant other/ committed relationships. The cubicle self has decided how a relationship should be from appearances, to activities, to how much time spent together, to how each party should behave, what the other person should and shouldn't say and do ... on and on. In other words, the cubicle self has lots of expectations and preconceived notions about how a relationship "should" be. Not to judge here what may or may not be helpful to some relationships; just noting the usually unspoken expectations that each party in a relationship is holding.

So, one day one or both of the persons goes seeking help for the relationship. Inspiration responds with great wisdom as to how to help the relationship. This always involves engaging one's True Self. So, one's True Self goes home and applies the help it has to offer and it often helps one part of the relationship, but another part is still not up to par (according to the cubicle perceptions), not up to one's expectations or the other party is resisting the help.

A point will be reached in any relationship inviting Inspiration in to help, where the false paradigm must be let go, so the Inspired Paradigm may enter. This is the point where most relationships break up and usually way before this point is reached. It is a crucial time to be handled with great wisdom — frequent pausing. One or both parties may decide to throw in the towel or one or both parties may decide to shift into the Inspired Paradigm. Keep in mind that this is a huge shift for it means the recognition and acceptance of literally, a new way of life. Not at a material level, though that may happen, but on a personal and interpersonal level. One's true personhood, the True Self begins to be more fully realized. This changes everything.

DO NOT BE AFRAID. Inspiration will give us all the Inspiration we want. It will not force Inspiration upon us that we do not want or are not ready for. The other party may not be ready for an Inspired relationship at the same time you are or one day he/she is ready and you are not and the next day you are ready and he/she is not, but there are the moments when you are both ready. It may be a flash of a moment, but the reality of that experience embeds itself in you. These are the moments we never forget because they are unforgettable; they are unforgettable because they came from our remembering our connectedness, which is infinite.

The question is, do you want to continue the cubicle relationship dance of "twist and shout" or are you willing to trust that Inspiration has set in motion something for you that far surpasses the steps of this dance.

LIVING HEALTH IS LIVING

Take off your dancing shoes for you have grown weary
and the soles are worn.
Now, rest your feet upon Inspired Ground —
Be rested and rest assured.
Living Health has arrived.

THIS WORLD
IS HERE
SO
YOU CAN HELP
1:1—NOW!

THIS WORLD IS HERE SO YOU CAN HELP 1:1—NOW!

TABLE OF CONTENTS

FOREWORD

WNYHOO–NOW! is an acronym for World Needs Your Help One-to-One — NOW! It is pronounced "winny-who-now" or however you want to say it! What is WNYHOO–NOW!? We are a nonprofit 501(c)(3) dba Pause For Inspiration. We hope to continue to offer various materials, programs and services — including this book — all for free. Visit our website: www.pauseforinspiration.org.

Let me share a few things that may be helpful in receiving this "Inspired To Be Truly Helpful" material and its being meaningful and useful in everyday life. Being Truly Helpful is seeing anew. Being Truly Helpful happens when someone is willing to open to Inspiration Within; this is why it is Truly Helpful. This is how WNYHOO–NOW! came into being. It does not refer to a particular way of behaving or right words to say. I am not providing instructions on how to walk, talk, dress, be nice, to use our common sense or how to be what we think is "spiritual". We each have full access to Inspiration Within, who will guide us in all areas of life 24/7. You see, I didn't brainstorm any of this material or sit down one day and decide to develop a program or write a book on how to inspire people to be truly helpful. One day I was simply open to experiencing peace of mind. I had recently written a series of stories about my practice of letting go of the judgmental mind and I was editing these stories for compilation in a book I was writing, *Visions of Illumination*.

MISSION
An Invitation to the whole world.
Pause For Inspiration in the midst of everyday life
Pause
Step Back
Step Aside
Let Inspiration Guide

Sitting outside at an outdoor café on a sunny, crisp October afternoon reading over my experiences and editing as needed, I paused a moment and looked up. My eyes fell upon a waitress in motion. As I observed her a moment, I noticed how she missed an opportunity to help a customer with something. No big deal really. Instead of going into judgement about how people just aren't paying attention and on and on with personal pet peeves, I returned to my editing when I heard a clear thought resounding in my mind, "SOMEONE NEEDS TO HELP THESE PEOPLE. THEY NEED TRAINING ON HOW TO BE HELPFUL." This thought was more than a passing thought or typical idea of my own. It bolted into my awareness as clear as day compelling my attention amidst my deep focus on finishing a project. I was Moved.

Immediately, I moved my pen from the left side of my notebook to the right page of my notebook and out came the words, "Inspired To Be Truly Helpful." I began furiously scribbling down the thoughts coming rapid fire. A whole program of sorts was unfolding before my eyes. I began laughing and was filled with joy as the thoughts hit the paper. There was a driving Force behind the words; a Force that knew what it was talking about and that Force was not me — that is, not the Mary I thought myself to be. Yet, this Force was clearly within me, connected to me and definitely knew me. This was Love. This was Joy. Lighthearted, clear, playful — with a wild sense of humor. A few pages into writing down what I was hearing, I began to get excited, thinking that this must be some kind of customer service training program. Oh gee, I thought, I can start my own business and go around to businesses and sell them on my customer service training program; that would be a pretty good job! But as I continued to write the meaning of the material was expanding beyond my expectations.

This "Voice" (not really an audible voice), inside my mind, was handing out ideas that were about a lot more than anything I ever heard of in a typical human resources training. It was busting myths about everything: politeness, behaviors, dress codes, handshakes, eye contact, corporate hierarchy, goal setting, communication skills, helpfulness, inspiration and even customers! Turns out, customers are not just those people buying things or consumers of services and products. They are needed to keep a business in business and much more. Customers are you and me. The Voice said to me, "We are all customers. And we are here (in the world) to provide one another with supreme customer service!" Then I saw my hand moving faster and faster and spilling out onto the paper were the words, "THIS IS FOR THE WHOLE WORLD."

What I thought was only a specialized customer service training program for innovative businesses, open-minded employers and employees, entrepreneurs and up and coming visionaries, was being shown to me as a great deal more than that! Inspiration was showing me a vision of service; giving service a whole new meaning. The fact that you and I are all here now at this particular time and space is no accident. You, simply by being a fellow human being, are my customer. And I, simply by being a fellow human being, am your customer! We are all here to help one–to–one. We all want peace of mind, right? Excellent customer service instills peace. If we want peace, start giving it. Stop complaining about the lack of peace in the world and be a person in the world experiencing and sharing peace.

Not only that, but the way we are going to help one–to–one and experience peace is by being willing to be open to Inspiration Within. What is Inspiration Within? Inspiration is the experience I just shared with you. A Vast Love exists within our mind, but it doesn't exist within the part of our mind that we are usually working from — sorry! This isn't to put down anything I already do or how I do it. Pause For Inspiration is here to lift up, transform and infuse life into our everyday thinking, doing and living. How? By offering you and me the opportunity to open up to and experience our Inspiring Self Heart∞Mind.

I am not psychic nor have I been specially created or gifted in that I hold some extraordinary powers that enabled me to receive this material. I am not a writer; I am willing to listen. Inspiration flows freely through the Inspiring Self Hearts and Minds of all — we need only pay attention.

Listen. Here is something I want you to hear. While listening and writing this material, I truly enjoyed the experience and felt graciously uplifted. Then I would stop and return to living my normal life in my normal cubicle self mind and began noticing myriad feelings arise about the material. Who does this Inspiring Self think it is anyway? I've got a good hold on my life and even if I do not, who does? Life is good enough. Inspiration is fine for special occasions and moments here and there, but I don't need Inspiration to move through everyday life stuff. That seems like a lot of work. After all, I am helpful enough all on my own. Rebelliousness began rising to the surface and I didn't want anything to do with my Inspiring Self or this material. Though this cubicle character could be a full caseload, at least I knew the routine. The outcome was up for grabs, but I held the cards and even if it seemed like a good hand or a bad hand, they were my cards! And, I'm not letting go of my cards.

It wasn't until I had the opportunity to begin presenting the material to people, which I did not want to do either, that I began seeing its value. Though I saw its value I still felt it was more trouble than it was worth. The cubicle self mind had kicked into full gear using fear as its engine. And "Why me?" Certainly Inspiration had the wrong person. I was all for being of service and moving along my "spiritual" path — whatever that means — but sharing this material with others seemed like a big undertaking that was not for me! I was to eventually find out that this "me-character" was going to have to step back — I was going to have to get out of my own way and be willing to see Another Way.

I was aware that this material clearly wasn't of my own making and was Truly Inspired. Yet, I also saw that sharing Inspiration comes with responsibility. The responsibility to practice what you teach and let go; let go of what people think — their approval or disapproval and let go of the outcome! Inspiration assured me in no uncertain terms saying, "WNYHOO–NOW! does not belong to you. Not only are you not supposed to "do" WNYHOO alone, you cannot do it alone. WNYHOO belongs to everyone." Thank God, what a relief!

This material showed up because I wanted something real. I wanted more than "that's life, deal with it." I wanted more than personal and worldly success. I wanted Love — The Real Love. I wanted peace of mind. I have experienced many instances of a Helpful Peace surrounding me. I have experienced timeless spans of being absorbed in Deep Peace; a Peace in which nothing and no one was missing. I wanted to share this experience, because even though the pull of the cubicle self who lives in fear of losing my loyalty was strong, I felt a stronger pull — the pull of the Peace that passes all understanding. I wanted more experiences of This Peace, for me, for you and for the world. I know This Peace is free to everyone because when I come face-to-face with it, everyone is present and we are all free. That is the nature of This Peace; it simply will not withhold Love from anyone — no matter what. It also will not force itself upon me as This Love completely respects my willingness. "Well," replied Inspiration, "You asked for a way to help others open to an experience of peace, joy and seeing anew. You asked for it Mary, and here it is." Ask and you shall receive in your giving one-to-one.

Here is what I am learning as I am willing to Pause For Inspiration in the midst of everyday life:

- ⊙ I am seeing how Inspiration does not necessarily Inspire the way I may think it should! Inspiration appears in relationships, situations, in thought, word and action in ways I do not expect or ever imagined. Though this material was an answer to a prayer, this is not what I ever saw the answer to my prayer being — ever!

- ⊙ I am seeing how this "me-character," the false self, (known as the "cubicle self" in this book) lives in fear of being exposed and at the same time wants to be the center of attention. That's a divided mind! Divided because it has no Center. Yet, it makes great efforts to be the Center even in the name of "Love."

- ⊙ I am seeing what a relief it is to step back from "me." This guy is exhausting. Even the me that wants to be spiritual, be helpful, do good in the world, accomplish, achieve — this me has quite an agenda — all centered around me!

- ⊙ I am seeing that there are still moments when I go "totally cubicle!"

- ⊙ I am seeing that it is one thing to receive Inspiration, it is a second thing to listen to Inspiration and it is a complete other third thing to follow! Following is where all the cubicle resistance shows up.

- ⊙ I am seeing that as I follow, I am no longer postponing Being Truly Helpful for some special occasion or special relationship. I am Being Truly Helpful while living my day-to-day life wherever and with whomever I find myself in the moment — as I Pause, Step Back, Step Aside and Let Inspiration Guide.

⊙ I am seeing that Being Truly Helpful is not what I have been thinking. Being Truly Helpful is seeing beyond who I think I am, who I think you are, who you think you are to seeing who you and I truly are through Eyes Who See — the sight of Inspiration Within. I need only get out of my own way.

⊙ I am seeing that as I am willing to allow Inspiration Within to guide how to be, where to go, what to do, I am connecting with people I would not have otherwise given a second glance and only good is coming forth. I am now truly connecting with those I thought I had been connected with — realness changes everything — real realness. I am laughing and loving like never before as I am willing to follow Inspiration Within.

⊙ I am seeing in myself and others how painful it is to be unwilling to extend love.

⊙ I am seeing the body in a more expansive way. As a potential communicator of Inspiration. Not an end in and of itself, but rather a means of sharing and following the wisdom of Inspiration Within—Inspiration In Motion!

⊙ I am seeing This Peace and experiencing This Peace. This Peace is the understanding I have been seeking.

All in all, I am beginning to see.

Peace be with you,

Mary Gerard Lenihan

THE BOTTOM LINE

. . . .

I have asked Inspiration Within, whom I experience as, The Mentor Within, to give me an introduction to Pause For Inspiration.

Mentor Within, give me an introduction to the book, Pause For Inspiration. Please. Thanks. An intro that is relevant to people so they can see how Inspiration Within functions in our everyday life in the world, through us. You know.

To my surprise, the introduction to the book showed up, in the form of a poem. Once again, Inspiration Within has given help in a way that I would not have done on my own! Here it is.

> Hear ye, Hear ye, oh face in the crowd
> A Constant Present Peace
> Is flowing around you now.
> This Peace is a Friend to you,
> A close friend indeed,
> A Friend you can be sure,
> Is well within your reach.
> Inspiration Within is our dear friend,
> Let us listen for This Wisdom
> Listen as one would listen
> For the arrival of a dear friend.
>
> How do you listen to such a Quiet One?
> How do hear a Whisper amidst the
> Quest, to get "it all" done?
> How do you know that what you hear
> Is This Whisper,
> And not your own, self-made fear?
>
> Inspiration Within is opening to you
> Through your Given Mind and Heart
> Helping you to do your part.
> Yes, Inspiration is revealing its Wisdom
> Through this you, that is you.
> Like a New Sky clearing a way through the clouds
> Inspiration's constant flow
> knows you, so you may know,
> That this you, that is you
> Is an Inspired flow.

Meet this you that is you
Open and do not close.
You are sure to reap what you sow
If you are sowing with One who knows.
This you, that is you, is not afraid to say what
    he thinks,
Not half mad or even on the blink.
This is your Inspired Self Heart∞Mind
Here to be more than occasionally kind.
Kindness is all right, it surely has its measure,
But the heart of this Inspired you, is the true treasure.

Inspiration will take your troubles, your worries
    and your woes,
Even take your joys, your twinkles and your foes.
Not to transform them or fix them up in the shop,
Nope, Inspiration has an Inspired Plan,
So you might want to stop.

While life has got you busy with work, fortune
    and/or fame
Your Inspired Self∞Mind is calling out your name.
Refereeing all your games, dismissing all your shames
Knowing for a fact, that no one is served in blame.
Love is here for a reason,
Putting an end to the seeming treason.
You have not been betrayed, but
You have been deceived
By this cubicle self's so-called absolute needs,
Pulling you this way and that
At the drop of a hat.
Be still in this moment,
Choose another way,
The way of Certainty
Calling you forth to truly see.
Give over to this Certainty
The darkness weighing on your mind.
Rest and let this Certainty
Rest the burdens on your mind.

The only mistake you have made
Is that you have forgotten who you are,
And in the midst of all the forgetting
You have raided the cookie jar.
So you are down to one or two cookies

And wondering what to do next,
I will give you a hint,
It is written in this text.
So, read on if you will
It will not take much time
And even better than that
Will not cost you one thin dime.

Some may think it cannot be worth much
If it does not cost a cent,
Well, I have good news for you,
This is Inspiration sent.
But if you are one
Who likes to pay,
Just remember one thing
Before you do or say.
We will take your donation
This we graciously accept,
Put it to good use,
Be sure it is well kept.
But the value of this book
Is not in how much it costs,
The value of this book
Is in its helping, all of us.
For it offers a great help to you,
And those in your midst.
It offers peace of mind
While checking off your lists.
So please do not put it on the shelf,
Hoping to get to it one day.
Do not imagine for a moment
That you already know what it has to say.
Please my dear friend,
See to it right away.
Remember, time is on your side —
Until it runs out.

So here is the deal,
The bottom line, if you will,
We all need help
And there is not much time left to kill.
I am speaking of Help,
From Inspiration Within.
While you may have been searching
For help around the bend,

Inspiration's Help is here and now,
Resting within.

Inspiration wants to Help you
Even give you a good laugh,
It asks nothing of you and
Is not condemning you in wrath.
So, unpack your bags
Take off your shoes,
You are not going anywhere —
At least not until
You pull up a chair.
For here you will pause,
And look on the inside.
Do not worry, do not fret
No one travels alone on This Ride.
It does not change a thing,
How your life appears thus far,
Inspiration has a plan for you,
And those hands in the cookie jar.

The bottom line is this:
Will you do your part;
I will do mine.
I am here to serve you,
If you are in the serving line.
Your part is simple
Never changes its tune,
It is your little willingness,
Which will be followed by a boon.
Willingness to what?
Well, get out of your own way
And listen to your Inspired Heart∞Mind,
On this One Fine Day.

What is the point,
What good will it do?
Whether it is the kids overwhelming you,
Your parents or your job in the zoo,
Or perhaps taxes, rent, mortgages too —
Relationship upheaval got you in a jam,
Got a headache over the daily scam,
Messages coming in, emails stacking up,
Giving your all to this overflowing cup —
Or maybe as you see it life is going well,

But is your neighbor feeling so swell?
If you would give Inspiration a chance,
All I am waiting for is your willing glance.

Life is filled with decisions
The moment the day begins
Turn towards Inspiration Within
Your True Next of Kin.
This True Kin of yours will not squabble
Over the past, will not ignore you
Or hate you for what you did or
Did not do last.
Ask of Inspiration Within anything at all,
You can be sure Inspiration
Hears the sound of your willingness,
And responds to your every call.

Listen,
You have an Inspired Mind,
And it is not airy fairy.
Airy fairy is putting your trust
In your cubicle mind,
Who is telling you that you are scary.
This cubicle self mind is
Full of hot air
Completely unaware
It is lost in the world's fair.

Here is the bottom line,
I am giving it to you again
For you may have forgotten
And I am your Friend.
There is a decision in this moment,
This one and the next,
And this decision that is yours
Is not to be taken in jest.
Do not get too serious though
For that will serve no one
Who is seeking to know.

Decide for your cubicle self
And here comes the wearies
Often followed by hearts sagging and teary.

Decide for your Inspired Self,
Help has arrived!
Breathe a sigh of relief
You are now free to thrive.
Your thriving helps another,
Now there is joy in your giving,
Giving what you are being Given
In the midst of your everyday living.

In giving from your Inspired Mind
You will now come to see,
That it truly is yours to use,
And has been given you for free.
The peace you are seeking is nowhere if not Within,
For the answers to your questions are
Resting with your True Friend.

Today is your day
And it does not end here.
While in your Inspired Mind
The horizon becomes clear.
Being present in this moment
There is no past to fear,
Inspiration's Presence in this moment
Is also in your future, dear friends.

So, Pause,
Step back,
Step aside too,
And Let Inspiration Guide.

**"Your Satisfaction Is Absolutely Guaranteed!
Or you can have your cubicle mind back."**

PAUSE

FOR INSPIRATION

WHAT IS
PAUSE FOR INSPIRATION?

An in-the-moment expression of INSPIRATION. The Pure Spirit of Peace and Helpfulness is pervading the universe as you connect with your INSPIRING SELF MIND and your INSPIRING SELF HEART. How? By BEING TRULY HELPFUL. Say, "So long," to your cubicle self who is busy thinking on its own in its cubicle, unable to see beyond its cubicle world.

Say, "Hello," to your Inspired Self who is patiently awaiting your attention and willingness to listen. Pause For Inspiration is a mission that begins in the heart of every willing mind. Being Truly Helpful is seeing through, above and beyond the cubicle self and into the Inspired Self. In this presence of heart and mind, you experience INSPIRATION. Allow Inspiration through you to Inspire the dispirited and experience your Inspiring Self Heart and Mind. As we give help in ways seen and unseen, so shall we receive help.

Remember,

YOU ARE A LIVING EXPRESSION OF INSPIRATION
IN THE WORLD!

CUBICLE SELF MIND

MISSION OF THE CUBICLE SELF

YEAH, i PRETTY MUCH AIM FOR THE STATUS QUO — WOE, WOE, WOE. My PROGRAMS AND SERVICES ARE FOCUSED ON KEEPING ALL THE CUBICLES IN THEIR PLACE. DO NOT STEP OUT OF THE CUBICLE! CHANGE AND ADVANCEMENT are ACCEPTABLE AS LONG AS IT REMAINS IN THE CUBICLE. PERMISSION SLIPS SIGNED BY YOUR CUBICLE SELF ARE REQUIRED FOR ANY SUCH CHANGES OR ADVANCEMENTS.

I will undoubtedly, eventually bring you

DISPIRITEDNESS, but THAT'S LIFE. Right?

SO, CAN I SIGN YOU UP?

INSPIRING SELF MIND

MISSION FOR THE INSPIRING SELF MIND!

I experience quality of life through the practice of Being Truly Helpful. Inspired programs and services Inspire awareness of our connectedness to our Inspiration Within and to one another.

I begin Inspiring the dispirited in everyday life because I am willing to be a living expression of Inspiration in the world!

Are you willing to do your part?

Your part is all you really can do. You cannot do someone else's part. No one else can do your part. What is your part?

Letting your mind be healed. Letting your heart be healed.
By Seeing with INSPIRATION

One–to–One

NOW!

MAY I HAVE YOUR ATTENTION PLEASE:

NOTICE TO ALL CUSTOMERS
(that is you and me)

If you live in this world, you do business in this world,
It is the business of living in the world. We are all customers in the
business of living in the world.

CUSTOMER SERVICE IS BEING TRULY HELPFUL — NOW!

We are in the business of customer service first and foremost.
Satisfied customers = Peace flowing in the business of living in the
world.

WANT MORE PEACE? PAUSE FOR INSPIRATION

Pause For Inspiration is here to help by Inspiring one another
to experience the joy of True Service; Service that comes from
Inspiration Inspires everyone. As customers, we feel uplifted
and don't even know why!

WE HAVE A GENUINE DESIRE TO SERVE.

How is this possible? Your Inspired self is here to Be Truly Helpful.

WHO IS THIS INSPIRED SELF?

The mind that has the light on. The mind whose communication
is Inspiration. Experience your Inspired Self for your Self!

WHO IS **Pause For Inspiration** FOR?

Everyone from the "top down," bottom up, behind the scene, on
the scene. Everyone plays a role keeping the wheel in motion.

WHO IS THIS TRAINING FOR?

You! That would be you! Yah, you!

One does not require training in customer service. One requires
willingness to Be Truly Helpful. Here is where training is required.

WHERE DID WILLINGNESS TO SERVE GO?

It never left; it simply got bogged down by too much thinking; sound familiar? Too much thinking blocks awareness of Inspiration. Being Inspired is not rocket science. It is not a gift only given to a precious few. You need not hold any special talents.

It is simply being willing to pause, get out of your own way and let your Inspired Self do what it does for a living — Inspire and Desire to help!

EVERYONE HAS AN INSPIRED SELF.

It is the you, in the now! Got that? Tap into your Inspiring Self Heart and your Inspiring Self Mind.

RECEIVE IN-THE-MOMENT DIRECTION:

DIRECTION ON WHAT?

- Keeping your eye on the goal.

  Oh, by the way, "What is the goal?"

  The goal is "to Be Truly Helpful."

HOW ELSE DOES YOUR INSPIRED SELF HELP?

- It directs you as to the next step towards the goal – that's just one step, one step at a time!

- Your Inspired Self guides communication with other "customers"; whether you are on the phone, writing an email or face-to-face.

Now, I know this all seems like common sense; aren't we already doing this kind of stuff? Well, yes, we are already setting goals, thinking that we are moving towards goals and communicating nonstop; the question is,

WHO IS SETTING YOUR GOALS?

Your cubicle self or your Inspired Self?

HOW ARE YOU GOING ABOUT ACHIEVING THOSE GOALS?

Are you cubicle-ized or Inspired?

Dispiritedness or Inspiration?

BEING TRULY HELPFUL IS ESSENTIAL TO THE BUSINESS OF LIVING IN THE WORLD, if we value peace of mind while we are living in the world with all the day-to-day challenges it brings.

When we serve our customers (this is one another), customers serve us — we receive help in return! It is like a mutual fund!

LOOKING FOR A GOOD INVESTMENT?

C   U   S   T   O   M   E   R   S

Invest in customers! What do you got to lose? Go ahead, trade a few shares.

"CUSTOMER" STANDS FOR:

C (SEE)

U (YOU)

S EEING

T HROUGH

O NE

M IND

E VERYONE'S

R EAL

S ELF

HERE IS THE RETURN ON YOUR INVESTMENT!

⊙ *PEACE OF MIND*

⊙ *Supreme Customer Service as I Recognize that to Give is also to Receive; it's a WIN-WIN for Everyone.*

⊙ *I Open to the Flow of My True Abundance in Inspiration; an Abundance that doesn't Wax and Wane Depending on the Circumstances.*

⊙ *Others Feel Inspired To Be Truly Helpful.*

⊙ *Being Focused on the Goal of Being Truly Helpful I have More Energy because I Am Receiving.*

⊙ *Giving is Replenishing. This Is Very Different than Only Being Focused on Getting Things Done which May Feel Like an Accomplishment at First, but Ends Up Being Depleting.*

⊙ *Productivity Increases because My Thoughts are Focused Rather than Wasting Time on Distractions.*

⊙ *I Am Saving Money, Time and Energy.*

⊙ *Communication, Communication, Communication – FINALLY! I Am More Clear and If Someone Else Is Not Clear, I Know What Questions to Ask to Gain Clarity.*

⊙ *I Feel Good – Inspiration is the Best Wellness.*

⊙ *It Prevent Errors and Accidents – the Inspired Self is Paying Attention.*

⊙ *I Experience My Inspired Self in All Aspects of Life: Work, Play, Relationships, Health*

And not last or least,

⊙ **I FEEL PURE JOY**

PURE JOY
FLOWS FROM INSPIRATION
INTO EVERYONE'S
INSPIRED SELF
TO BE TRULY HELPFUL.

Am I Making This Up?

How do I know this material came forth from Inspiration Within? How do I know I didn't make this all up? I have come to know this cubicle mind extremely well for I have observed it in myself and others in action, in words and in thoughts. I have invited Inspiration Within to show me this cubicle mind so I can recognize its ways and woes. I know its twists and turns and all the many detours and deviations it takes, often in the name of "love" or "kindness" or "helpfulness" or "good intentions." I know its nature and I know it to be false. The cubicle mind is not a bad person; it simply does not know any better. It does not know any better because it does not know Love.

How do I know the cubicle nature to be a false nature? I have experienced my True Nature. I have seen the True Nature of others. And this is an indescribable hope and completeness that you will need to experience for yourself. It may seem that one does not need "hope" if one is complete, yet we do. We need to be hopeful for those who have yet to experience their completeness in Love. We need to remain hopeful for ourselves who will undoubtedly fall again and again into our false nature. Being hopeful is our willingness to receive help and give help.

Awareness of the presence of Inspiration Within is available to everyone who wants this experience. Inspiration is not a grand master in the sky speaking to only a precious few. Love is everything and for everyone, otherwise it is not Love. Fear comes in the forms of many different voices saying many different things, often contradictory or fear shows up as consistent unawareness. Love is consistently sharing one absolute — LOVE.

Inspire the Dispirited —
Listen and Follow

Inspiration Within is within each one of us. From your cup of morning "Joe" to your cooking, cleaning, driving, taking care of, work force world and even deep into the night while you are asleep.

How does one come to recognize this "Voice" if you will? Listen. Inspiration Within is communicating; you are to practice listening! You practiced how to learn to ride a bike, didn't you? This is not magic. Your part is essential as an instrument of Inspiration Within AND please do not make up your own part without listening as this is unhelpful.

Here is the most excellent thing about listening to and following Inspiration Within: you become a "Willing Vessel" of this Love. This is how you Inspire the dispirited, which includes yourself!

The following is a practice in listening, following and Inspiring the dispirited.

INSPIRING THE DISPIRITED
Healing One–to–One

In all of our relationships, whether a moment in passing, the passing of a lifetime or somewhere in between, is the opportunity for dispiriting one another or Inspiring one another. We are either forgetting who we are or remembering who we are. To be dispirited is to have forgotten who I am. To forget who I am is to be without purpose no matter how busy I may keep.

Being Inspired is being who I truly am for I am Inspired.

Who I am is my purpose.

Who I am is a living expression of Inspiration in the world.

THE "P E A R L"

. . . .

"a practice in Inspiring the dispirited"

Pause your mind. Be still on the inside.
Still your body if needed.

Express your willingness to open to Inspiration
Within; *"I am willing."*

Allow Awareness to shift to Inspiration's Presence
within you.

Rest with a One-Pointed focus on This Presence.
Slow down. Receive.

Listen and Follow This Wisdom being
revealed to you.

. . . .

STAY AWARE
OF BEING CONNECTED

If you become distracted, STAY AWARE OF BEING CONNECTED:

Notice you are distracted.

Pause.

Return to your willingness to rest in a One-Pointed focus
on Inspiration *Within.*

Listen and Follow.

Seeing Inspiration

Listening to and following Inspiration will inevitably lead to an experience of being connected within yourself, to others and to This Peace. How do you know you are listening to the Wisdom of Inspiration and not just your own well-meaning ideas? Here are some guidelines to help you recognize Inspiration Within:

First, Inspiration Within is immaculate; there is not a speck of fear upon it. In the moments of awareness of This Love there is no fear. There is only Love.

Second, Inspiration Within is only Truly Helpful. You are opened to being an instrument of Inspiration in the world — instead dispiritedness.

Third, Inspiration Within extends only Love; not the cubicle version of "love," rather, Real Love. You will know the difference if you are willing to look at your motivations and desired outcomes.

Fourth, in the awareness of Inspiration Within, cubicle mind dispiriting perceptions fall away.

Fifth, Inspiration Within provides a way to move through cubicle pain and suffering. This Love is our Companion and Helper through and out of our cubicle messes.

Sixth, Inspiration Within leads everyone into peace; no one is left behind except by one's own choice for fear instead of Love. You are always free to choose again.

Seventh, Inspiration Within is giving a constant supply of Infinite Love, sufficient for all your seeming deficiencies.

PAUSE FOR INSPIRATION

Eighth, Inspiration Within hears your sound of willingness before you do and is listening to your every call. Don't be surprised if you call upon Inspiration and find This Presence has been with you all along.

Ninth, Inspiration Within walks with you always and in all ways; even though you may not feel This Presence, trust that Love is with you. Where else would Love be?

Tenth, Inspiration Within speaks directly, with clarity and without fear. The cubicle mind may very well react with fear to This Love because it feels a threat to its cubicle control. The cubicle mind has grown accustomed to your allegiance and Love's entrance may pose a threat. On the other hand, you may choose to be open instead of closing in fear and welcome an encounter with Inspiration Within.

Eleventh, Inspiration Within will not override your choice for ego, yet it rides with you wherever you go in case you decide to change your mind.

Twelfth, Inspiration Within is the quiet whisper in your Inspired Heart∞Mind calling you into awareness of who you truly are and your true purpose. For it is in awareness of who you truly are that your true purpose is revealed. Your purpose is to be who you truly are. Ask Inspiration Within, "Who am I?" and listen for the answer. Now you will see your purpose. Now you will also know what this world is for.

HOW WNYHOO–NOW! CAME TO BE

. . . .

One moment in time a willing mind and an open heart in their one desire to be Inspired, looked around the world and heard the Thought,

"SOMEONE NEEDS TO HELP THESE PEOPLE!

THEY NEED TRAINING ON

HOW TO BE HELPFUL!"

The moment this Thought was heard

WNYHOO–NOW!

World Needs Your Help One-to-One—NOW!

BEGAN!

A few moments down the road another Thought was Given,

"THIS IS FOR THE WHOLE WORLD."

Inspiring Self Mind?

Cubicle Self Mind?

INSPIRING SELF MIND

What is the Inspiring Self Mind ?

CUBICLE SELF MIND
What is the cubicle self mind?

THE INSPIRING SELF MIND IS THE PART OF OUR MIND
THAT IS ILLUMINATED.

The cubicle self mind
is the part of our mind
that is in the dark.

THE INSPIRING SELF MIND IS AWARE.

The cubicle self mind
is unaware.

THE INSPIRING SELF MIND NAVIGATES
and WE REACH OUR GOAL.

The cubicle self mind
is lost in a maze of its
own shifting goals.

THE INSPIRING SELF MIND SEES ITS PART IN THE WHOLE.

The cubicle self mind
sees only the cubicle
and all of its parts.

THE INSPIRING SELF MIND AIMS FOR PEACE.

The cubicle self mind
aims for conflict.

THE INSPIRING SELF MIND IS NOT A NEW AND IMPROVED

cubicle self mind!

THE INSPIRING SELF MIND IS CLEAR OF ITS OWN IDENTITY AS
IT IS CONNECTED TO INSPIRATION, THEREFORE IT IS CLEARLY
IN NO NEED OF IMPROVEMENT!

The cubicle self mind
may attempt self-
improvement and
expanding its horizons,
but no matter where it
goes, what it does, or
what it says it never leaves
the cubicle self mind; It
can't see beyond
the cubicle, so
where would it go?

WE DO NOT NEED a cubicle self that is more educated,
more experienced, richer, wiser, good looking, spiritual, holy
and with a new and improved self-esteem!

REMEMBER attempting to improve the cubicle self is a distraction

from paying attention to the

INSPIRED SELF.

Go ahead, go back to school, make that investment, exercise,
get your hair done . . .

This is not to undo any of these things we all do day in
and day out.

It is opening to receiving

DIRECTION FROM THE INSPIRING SELF MIND

PRIOR TO AND WHILE IN THE MIDST OF

setting our schedule, doing our routine, goal setting and living in
the world.

TAKE

A

BREATH

PAUSE HERE

JUST

BE

Inspiring Self Heart?
Cubicle Self Heart?

INSPIRING SELF HEART:

What is the *Inspiring Self Heart?*

CUBICLE SELF HEART:

What is the cubicle self heart?

The cubicle self heart takes itself way too seriously.

The Inspiring Self Heart *knows that seriousness leads to hardening of the heart.* It is whimsical and light hearted.

The cubicle self heart has no room for gratitude.

The Inspiring Self Heart *is a room full of gratitude.*

The cubicle self heart is on lockdown.

The Inspiring Self Heart *is open.*

The cubicle self heart desires things.

The Inspiring Self Heart *desires to be helpful.*

The cubicle self heart sees the world as its foe or potential conquest.

The Inspiring Self Heart *sees the world as its playground and the land upon which to serve.*

The cubicle self heart
allies itself with conflict.

The Inspiring Self Heart *is aligned with peace.*

The cubicle self heart
takes.

The Inspiring Self Heart *gives.*

The cubicle self heart
shields.

The Inspiring Self Heart *receives.*

The cubicle self heart
hoards.

The Inspiring Self Heart *shares.*

The cubicle self heart
counts its losses.

The Inspiring Self Heart *shares its gains.*

The cubicle self heart
seeks passion.

The Inspiring Self Heart *is passion.*

The cubicle self heart
guesses.

The Inspiring Self Heart *knows.*

The cubicle self heart
lies.

The Inspiring Self Heart *is wise.*

The cubicle self heart
is down and out.

The Inspiring Self Heart *is within and without.*

WHICH HEART
IS LIVING
YOUR LIFE?

The INSPIRING SELF HEART∞MIND
Merge as One
In Inspiration

GET IN ON THIS MERGER
AND
REAP THE REWARDS — NOW!

THE MERGER

Imagine a sculpture of the cubicle self mind — what does it look like? Look at it. See yourself walking towards this structure and entering through the cubicle door. Once inside the cubicle mind, allow cubicle thoughts of self-judgment, judgment of others and self-limiting beliefs to come into your mind.

Notice what you are feeling — feel it.

This is the cubicle heart with its cubicle feelings ranging from numbness to rage and every-thing in between.

Ask yourself, "Is this how I want to experience life?

Numb or filled with rage and everything in between?

If your answer is, "No," smile upon yourself for you have just stepped towards willingness to experience INSPIRATION!

Say to yourself,

"I am willing to experience INSPIRATION.

I trust my INSPIRING SELF HEART∞MIND

is here with me now."

Release your cubicle judgments and limiting beliefs; let go of your cubicle heart cubicle feelings,

Whatever they may be.

Lay them down into the Pure Spirit of Peace.

DO NOT BE AFRAID. LET GO.

Be Present with your experience.

Be open to peace.

No effort. No force. Trust Peace.

Be with your experience.

SO LONG AND HELLO

WNYHOO — NOW!

World Needs Your Help

One–to–One — NOW!

BEING TRULY HELPFUL

HERE AND NOW.

TODAY,

RIGHT HERE IN MIDST OF

EVERYDAY LIVING.

NO EXTRA TIME.

NO SPECIAL PLACE TO BE.

ALL IT TAKES IS YOUR

WILLINGNESS

TO RELEASE THE

cubicle self into INSPIRATION

AND LISTEN TO ITS REPLACEMENT —

YOUR INSPIRING SELF.

WNYHOO — NOW!

IS HERE TO HELP YOU

DO YOUR PART IN HELPING THE WORLD.

AS YOU DO YOUR PART,

YOU INSPIRE OTHERS TO DO THEIR PART

AND YOU ARE INSPIRED IN RETURN!

TOGETHER WE ARE HEALING THE WORLD

IN WAYS SEEN AND UNSEEN.

OPENING TO THE INSPIRATION

OF OUR INSPIRING SELF

HELPS US HELP THE WORLD.

HERE AND NOW

IN EXTENDING HELP, WE RECEIVE HELP.

EXPERIENCE IT FOR YOURSELF!

YOUR INSPIRED SELF IS

INSPIRED TO BE TRULY HELPFUL NOW!

INSPIRATION FLOWS THROUGH EVERY

INSPIRED SELF NATURALLY

MOMENT–TO–MOMENT

WITHOUT OUR HAVING TO MAKE IT HAPPEN.

IT IS ALREADY HAPPENING RIGHT HERE.

WHERE IS HERE?

HERE IS NOW.

WHERE IS NOW?

IS IT ON YOUR WATCH? YOUR CELL PHONE?

YOUR COMPUTER?

NOPE.... NONE OF THESE!

NOW IS WITHIN YOUR MIND;

NOW IS WITHIN YOUR HEART!

PAUSE AND LISTEN

TO YOUR INSPIRED SELF.

So long to the cubicle self who is busy repeating the past and rehearsing for the future based
on its past performances!

*So long to the cubicle self who can't see beyond
the cubicle even standing on its tippy toes!*

HELLO TO YOUR INSPIRING SELF MIND

SEEING THROUGH THE

VISION OF INSPIRATION.

HELLO TO YOUR INSPIRING SELF HEART

KNOWING THE PEACE INSPIRATION IS.

WNYHOO — NOW!

ALL OF US HAVE A PART

WHETHER WE KNOW IT OR NOT

SIMPLY BECAUSE WE ARE HERE NOW.

Our being right here, right now is no accident.

You have a purpose.

WILL YOU DO YOUR PART — NOW?

Everyone has an Inspired Self.

If you don't believe this to be so,

Just wait.

HELP IS ON THE WAY!

WHY "WORLD"?

WHY WNYHOO?

WHY DOES THE WORLD NEED YOUR HELP ONE-TO-ONE?

WHY NOW?

Let's Begin with the "WORLD."

DON'T THINK THE WORLD NEEDS YOUR HELP?

> Such is the sorrowful saga of the cubicle self mind who sees no one in need of help for it has mirrored the walls, ceiling and floor of the cubicle and only sees itself; whether busy admiring itself or degrading itself. Either way the cubicle self mind sees only its own reflection and the cubicle self heart hears only its own sighs.

"KNOCK, KNOCK," says the Inspired Self.

> "Who's There?" says the cubicle self.

"It is I," answers the Inspired Self.

> "I who?" asks the cubicle self.

"I am your Inspired Self.

Why are you looking for Life amidst your own reflections?

You see, the cubicle self is looking for Life where none can be found, for the Life you seek, is Within your

Inspired Self."

As we begin helping the world, the world actually begins to look different. We begin experiencing more peace and less conflict — and when we see conflict we know we want to choose

Peace Instead of This —

and it is this choice within our mind and heart that changes

how we respond to conflict.

WHY "NEEDS"?

. . . .

NEEDS — WHY "NEEDS"?

The cubicle self hears the word "needs" and immediately asks, **"What's in it for me?"**

It asks this question because:

> First, it is living in lack — It feels its needs are already not being met so it isn't interested in helping with anyone else's needs.

> Secondly, it asks this question as a defense because it truly has nothing to give for it is running on empty.

HERE IS THE CUBICLE MINDSET:

> I DON'T HAVE WHAT I WANT. WHAT I DO HAVE IS NOT WHAT I WANT.

> I WANT MORE OF SOMETHING LIKE WHAT I HAVE, BUT A DIFFERENT VERSION OF IT THAT'S SOMEHOW BETTER.

> I CAN'T FIND WHAT I WANT, BUT I'LL KEEP LOOKING.

"Do you think the world needs peace
as much as you do?
Do you want to give it to the world
as much as you want to receive it?

For unless you do,
you will not receive it."

. . . .

The world needs help
because we need help
and the only way
we are going to get
the help we need
is by helping the world
one-to-one!

WHY "YOUR"?

YOUR — WHY "YOUR"?

This is not about Aunt Tootsie, coworker Mike, Uncle Penelope, your husband, wife, partner, friend, enemy, butcher, in-laws or next door neighbor changing. How many times have you thought, "SO and SO really needs to change."

THE cubicle self mind

WANTS EVERYBODY ELSE TO GET THEIR DUCKS IN A ROW, GET THEIR ACT TOGETHER, STRAIGHTEN UP, SIT DOWN, DO THIS THAT WAY, DO THAT THIS WAY, ETC.

MARY SHARES

GUESS WHO IS NOW SO AND SO? ME!

YES, I AM SO AND SO.

AND EACH TIME YOU ARE WILLING,

YOU ARE SO AND SO!

THE IRONY IS that often people and situations change for the better in ways I could have never forced upon them, WHEN I CHANGE!

AS I AWAKEN TO INSPIRATION IN MY MIND, THESE PEOPLE WHO ONCE SEEMED TO BE THE CAUSE OF MY HAIR STANDING ON END

NO LONGER SEEM SO THREATENING.

I CAN CHOOSE TO SEE THE TRUTH ABOUT THEM, WHICH IS THE PEACE WITHIN THEM, WHETHER THEY SEE IT OR NOT.

WHY "HELP"?

HELP—WHY "HELP"?

WHAT IS BEING TRULY HELPFUL?

Not what you may think.

Yes, this is volunteer work.

However, you are not volunteering to go to some special place, at some special time and do some special thing.

Of course, all of that is just fine,

Though WNYHOO — NOW!

Is a different kind of volunteering,

A different kind of help.

WNYHOO — NOW!

Is volunteering your Inspired Self to Direct your path and Lead the way

Through each and every day.

Of course, there will be many obstacles

To such an endeavor because

the cubicle self

prefers to direct and lead our lives,

For it likes to keep us and others

"in check"

"in line"

"in control"

"in the cubicle"

Etc.

"DO NOT STEP OUT OF THE CUBICLE"

The cubicle self feels familiarity in the cubicle and is able to keep tabs and know the score; which keeps changing, so it expends a lot of energy staying on top of the score!

No WNYHOO happening here, folks!

This makes for fear and the various forms fear takes; here's a few:

greed □ hatred □ dislike □ depression □ jealousy □ envy □ guilt □ unforgiveness □ judg- ment □ gossip □ denial □ lack □ perfectionism □ war □ isolation □ illness □ resistance □ addic- tion □ anger □ imbalance □ disharmony □ false happiness □ superficiality □ unworthiness □ brokenness □ lying □ making excuses □ chaos □ exclusion □ and last but not least, poor customer service!

What Is Being Truly Helpful?

Being Truly Helpful happens as I am WILLING to see you with my Inspiring Self Mind and Heart.

In this moment of willingness, the peace of INSPIRATION is naturally extended.

NOW I feel INSPIRED because I am receiving INSPIRATION by giving it.

I haven't lost anything in my giving; there has been no sacrifice of any kind, because Inspiration is Infinite.

IT DOESN'T STOP HERE —

As I am now seeing you with my Inspired Self, You are now INSPIRED, whether you know it or not.

In an unforeseen moment, having been seen truly, you will be moved to look upon another truly; in this moment, INSPIRATION is extended and you will experience your Inspired Self.

Thus, my willingness begins a chain of INSPIRATION ONE–TO–ONE

BRINGING HEALING TO THE WORLD!

HOW IS THIS HEALING?

IT AWAKENS US TO OUR SENSE OF CONNECTEDNESS; TO OUR SELVES, AND TO ONE ANOTHER. TO INSPIRATION. WE ARE MOVED FROM BELIEVING WE ARE SEPARATE TO EXPERIENCING WE ARE CONNECTED.

> > >

IN AWARENESS OF OUR CONNECTEDNESS
INSPIRATION IS INSPIRING THE DISPIRITED!

This experience in and of itself is Life-giving in ways seen and unseen.

Little do we know, nor do we need to know, how Inspiration works in the lives of all through our little willingness.

WE ARE BEING
INSPIRED TO BE TRULY HELPFUL!

NOTE:

INSPIRATION WILL INSPIRE US IN MYRIAD WAYS THAT WE WILL RECOGNIZE THROUGH PEACE;

INSPIRATION IS NOT MYSTERIOUS!

WE MAY BE MOVED TO SAY OR DO SOMETHING
OR SIMPLY TO SEE ANEW;

REMEMBER,

THE POWER OF YOUR

INSPIRING SELF HEART AND MIND

IS REAL!

BUT YOU WON'T KNOW,
UNTIL YOU ARE WILLING TO STEP BACK
FROM YOUR CUBICLE SO-CALLED POWER
AND EXPERIENCE THE REAL THING.

WHY "ONE-TO-ONE"?

We do not realize
just how much in Need of help we are,
until we help Someone else —

It is in helping Another that we receive the Help we need —

> this is not about giving everything up as a
> plan to get something in return at some later
> time — that is a **cubicle line of thought**!

There is no bargaining with INSPIRATION —

Rather, as we Give truly, another Receives whether they
notice it or not, and in another's Receiving they Give to us
and now we Receive!

(This is because nothing blocks the flow of Inspiration;
it always penetrates the cubicle darkness, however it is always
your decision to release the darkness and be aware of the peace
that is flowing within; Inspiration will not interfere with your
choices.)

Inspiration Within
is infinitely flowing—
whether you are aware of
This Flow or not—
∞

PAUSE FOR INSPIRATION

137

A CIRCLE OF GIVING AND RECEIVING

KNOCK, KNOCK

WHO'S THERE?

A HELPER

A HELPER WHO?

A HELPER FOR YOU!

We all have helpers in this world —

LOOK AROUND YOU RIGHT NOW —

Everyone here is your helper and

You are their helper!

We teach one another how to be truly helpful
by being truly helpful ourselves ~
Inspiration, through our Inspiring Self Heart and Mind shines
away the darkness of the cubicle heart and mind in another
and this
Awakens her or him to the Light within ~

Inspiration is a Light shining away the cubicle shadows ~

Now we see Inspiration flowing through others ~

And we are Inspired ~

INSPIRATION IS THE HELP WE SEEK,

BUT IT CANNOT BE FOUND BY THE CUBICLE MIND

IN THE CUBICLE WORLD.

YOU SEE, INSPIRATION IS NOT BOUND WITHN THE CUBICLE.

~

INSPIRATION ROAMS FREELY AND INFINITELY THROUGH

THE INSPIRING THOUGHTS AND HEART SILENCE

OF OUR INSPIRED SELF.

EVERY MOMENT IS AN OPPORTUNITY TO SEE ANEW,

TO HEAR A CALL FOR LOVE AND RESPOND.

~~~~~ MARY SHARES ~~~~~

Though in responding I may not receive any

accolades, awards, degrees,

certificates or public recognition,

I tell you this.

I have experienced these things

in and of the world,

and they in no way come near

the Indescribable peace, joy and satisfaction

I experience

as I am resting in the presence

of Inspiration.

ABSOLUTE SATISFACTION

A SHORT STORY

I am walking down the road one summer afternoon feeling a bit out of sync. My head is drooping down, eyes staring at my feet as if they hold some enlightened solution to my discord. I call upon Inspiration, the Pure Spirit of Peace, for help. Scanning my emotions with radar accuracy to assess exactly what it is I am feeling, I feel it, and I say to Inspiration "I feel dissatisfied." Just a twinge of dissatisfaction gnawing beneath the surface. "Hmm," I speak further to Inspiration Within, "What is this about? What would you have me do about this?" My head still hanging down, eyes glued to the sidewalk, I try to unscramble the emotional radar screen and decipher my dissatisfaction. Clueless in my deciphering, I feel my head lifting and I notice I am walking by a deli that has been on this same corner for 40 years; a deli I have moseyed by many, many times. Inspiration has sent me a sign, literally!

My mind drops open as my eyes fall upon a sign in their window; a sign that has been there all these years. A sign I have never seen. A sign that takes up one third of the storefront!

It says:

YOUR SATISFACTION IS ABSOLUTELY GUARANTEED!

I laugh. There you have it! My dissatisfaction was deciphered by being eliminated! Inspiration heard my call for help and answered. Inspiration lifted my head and guided my eyes to see what It would have me see. My Inspired Self is not suffering from dissatisfaction. My Inspired Self is satisfied and backs its satisfaction with a guarantee! I had to laugh to ever believe that I was unworthy of absolute satisfaction!

WHY "NOW"?

. . . .

NOW—WHY "NOW"?

Contrary to cubicle belief, we truly have nothing better to do!

Yes, we may schedule times to be truly helpful in the future — but, let us not overlook opportunities to be truly helpful RIGHT HERE, RIGHT NOW.

Be in your Inspiring Self Heart and Mind while scheduling future appointments!

MARY SHARES

A SHORT STORY

A typical day awaits me. My "To Do" list quickly becoming a "Why didn't you get this done yesterday list?" My cubicle self was ramping up its guilt as I barely hear in the back of my mind something like, "You lazy good for nothing. Why can't you get all this stuff done once and for all?" As if there is a "once and for all" in our nonstop do more world. If I had to spend the rest of my day doing, how was I supposed to fit time in for simply being? I had put being time at the bottom of my "To Do" list. Well, I had enough practice at doing while not being; that is doing while being completely unaware that I even have a being. It is a hateful way to treat myself and others. I decided — this is key by the way, realizing that the decision is mine — that I will not spend this day in a semi-conscious state riding the "Todomobile." So, I take a breath, call upon Inspiration Within for help staying connected to my Inspired Self and dial my dentist's office to make an appointment. The receptionist and I shared an uplifting connection. I felt her wishing me a good day at the end of our call to be truly genuine. By the sound of her voice, she felt uplifted as well.

BEING TRULY HELPFUL IS SO SIMPLE!

Imagine if our days were strung together by more of these kind of experiences instead of rushing, conflict and more rushing, piled atop more conflict.

> > >

. . . .

CLEAR YOUR MIND

I am not condoning just being nice. The Inspired Self is not focused on populating the world with more nice people. Nothing against nice people! The Inspired Self is real; the world needs more real people — people who know who they Truly are and are dedicated to seeing others for who they Truly are and helping others come into the awareness of who they Truly are — through seeing beyond appearances — seeing the being who is quietly resting behind the doing.

NO ORDINARY DEAL

· ·

IT MAY BE OBVIOUS TO YOU BY NOW

That this is no typical, superficial idea.
No dos and don'ts, costumes, make-up, phony smiles,
etiquette, how to walk, talk and dress.

No one really wants to go through life faking it;
customers can tell the difference (remember, we are all customers);

You know the difference between real and unreal.

Are you jumping for joy listening to external "experts" giving
advice about living a better life in a better world.

We have heard it all before and the world doesn't seem to be
getting better; and life seems more complicated than ever!

Even if the latest research about self-improvement is something
new, tomorrow the research will discredit itself with different
results.

The cubicle self mind isn't new
and it isn't Inspired.

ARE YOU WILLING TO BE INSPIRED?

DO YOU WANT TO BE INSPIRED?

Go ahead, take a moment and ask yourself,

"WHAT DO I REALLY WANT?"

IF IT'S PEACE OF MIND YOU'RE AFTER,

PAUSE FOR INSPIRATION
HAS ARRIVED — AND NOT A MOMENT TOO SOON!

World Needs Your Help One–to–One — NOW!

TIME IS A WASTIN'!

WE CAN STOP COMPLAINING THAT WE
DO NOT HAVE ENOUGH TIME

AND

BE HAPPY WITH THE TIME WE HAVE.

WE WILL BE HAPPY WITH THE TIME WE HAVE,
WHEN WE BEGIN USING IT WISELY —

BY BEING TRULY HELPFUL!

THE REASON WE FEEL LIKE WE NEVER HAVE ENOUGH TIME IS BECAUSE WE ARE NOT USING TIME FOR ITS HIGHEST PURPOSE.

YOU WILL DISCOVER
THAT IN YOUR BEING TRULY HELPFUL
IT IS AS IF TIME STANDS STILL,

BECAUSE EVEN WHILE THE CLOCK IS MOVING
INSPIRATION IS WORKING
IN THE STILLNESS OF YOUR HEART.

IF YOU WANT TO GET OFF THE CLOCK,

LISTEN

TO YOUR INSPIRED SELF.

INSPIRATION IS TIMELESS WISDOM
FLOWING THROUGH YOU!

NEED A VACATION?

FIGURING THAT YOU ARE ALREADY
"HELPFUL ENOUGH?"

THANK YOU FOR YOUR HELP.

NOW,

Let us take our "acts of kindness" and "service"
to Whole a new level.

While we are climbing the ladder of success, looking for the ladder
of success or hanging by one arm from the ladder of success, let
Inspiration take our everyday lives to the top of the ladder right
now one Inspiring moment at a time, one Inspiring thought at a
time.

Inspiration will help us do just this.

~~~~~~~~~~~~~~~~~ MARY SHARES ~~~~~~~~~~~~~~~~~

A simple act of opening the door for someone
with a smile

moves from social courtesy or being nice,
to being Inspiring, simply by being present in our awareness.

In this awareness INSPIRATION is flowing
through us and being extended to others in ways often

beyond words,

beyond explanation.

yet, not beyond experience.

You are beginning to experience your very nature differently.

You begin experiencing others differently.

A door within your mind is opening
to a vast reality

that we have been seemingly completely out of touch with —

it is like going on a vacation
only we don't have to physically travel anywhere!

Oh, I like that — no packing!

BE AWARE —

the cubicle self mind is easily offended by talk of Inspiration or any thought which does not adhere to its

CUBICLE SEPARATION DECLARATION!

Any possibilities which appear to threaten the very existence of the cubicle self mind drive the cubicle self mind right up the cubicle!

PAUSE FOR INSPIRATION
IS NOT HERE TO TEACH NEW BEHAVIORS, TRENDS AND TRICKS. AFTER ALL, WE DON'T LIKE TO BE TOLD HOW TO BEHAVE

EVEN IF IT COMES WITH A FREE LUNCH!

BY THE WAY

THERE ARE TWO REASONS THE CUBICLE SELF DOES NOT LIKE TO BE TOLD HOW TO BEHAVE:

REASON ONE:

THE CUBICLE SELF WANTS TO BE THE AUTHORITY

Here we go again, some lady telling me to button up, straighten up and speak up; dress up, don't look down, give a firm handshake, tone up, slim down, don't blink, smile — not too big, look'em in the eye, don't stare, look

interesting, look interested, ask questions, be a
good listener, write back, keep your eye on the
time, don't be late, don't be too early, be right
on time . . .

The closed thinking of the dispirited self wants to be our authority,
our Inspiration even!

Imagine that!

The dispirited self is blocking our awareness of Inspiration and
Inspiration is the highest authority!

But the cubicle self mind wants to be its own boss.

It has built its own house and is going to live in it, even if it did
forget to put in any doors or windows —

oops!

SEE WHAT HAPPENS WHEN YOU WANT

TO BE YOUR OWN BOSS!

AN AUTHORITY IS A RELIABLE SOURCE —

WOULD YOU HIRE A CUBICLE MAKER TO

CREATE AN INSPIRED SPHERE?

~~~~~~~~~~~~~ MARY SHARES ~~~~~~~~~~~~~

*AS I AM WILLING TO LET INSPIRATION BE MY TEACHER THROUGH
MY INSPIRED SELF, I SEE THAT I WOULD NEVER WANT THE CUBICLE
SELF IN A POSITION OF AUTHORITY— IT IS NOT A RELIABLE SOURCE
BECAUSE ITS SOURCE IS ITS SELF-MADE CUBICLE SELF!*

PAUSE FOR INSPIRATION
IS BREAKING FREE OF THE CUBICLE SELF!

PAUSE FOR INSPIRATION IS NOT ABOUT CHANGING

YOUR cubicle self;

IT IS ABOUT RECOGNIZING YOUR INSPIRED SELF MAYBE FOR THE FIRST TIME!

AHH, FREEDOM..........

REASON TWO

That we don't like being told how to behave.
Is because we think

WE KNOW WE KNOW.

The cubicle self thinks it knows mostly everything and is only willing to learn anything "new" that is in line with what it already thinks, hence it never really learns anything at all!

Repeating past learning, albeit in new forms, the cubicle self appears to be learning something new and gaining information, while remaining stagnant in old, unhelpful beliefs and attitudes.

Yes, new skills may be developed, but you have limited the use of these new skills if they are put in the hands of the cubicle self.

In the realm of Inspiration, "to learn" means "to correct"; that is, to unlearn any "mislearning," so to speak, that has occurred over time, in order to uncover the Truly Helpful knowledge beneath.

Being its own authority, the cubicle self is resistant to correction, as it may be corrected right out of the boss's chair!

DO NOT BE AFRAID

Do Not Fear the cubicle self.

Though it is highly skillful at doing what it does best — embedding dispiritedness — it is really not such a bad fellow.

The cubicle self is simply misguided, ignorant — meaning, it doesn't know any better. We needn't cut it off or tear it down or ignore it. Be aware of your cubicle self so as not to be misled into dispiritedness.

This doesn't mean you won't have low moments at times. Living in a world where most of us idolize the cubicle self, we are bound to fall into dispiritedness.

But, once again,

DO NOT BE AFRAID.

CALL UPON THE PURE SPIRIT OF PEACE AND RECEIVE THE HELPFUL PEACE IT IS CONSTANTLY SERVING.

LET PEACE BE YOUR AUTHORITY.

LET PEACE TEACH YOU WHAT YOU NEED TO KNOW TO LIVE IN PEACE.

LET PEACE TEACH YOU

HOW TO BE HELPFUL.

DO NOT FEAR THE CUBICLE SELF.

SEE IT FOR WHAT IT IS, THE SELF WHO DOES NOT KNOW LOVE, AND

GIVE IT TO PEACE.

The fact is you don't need to be told how to behave,
nor do you need to think you already know how to behave,
because you already know how to serve!

Our behavior is an extension of our willingness to serve or not to serve.

As you are willing to connect with your INSPIRED SELF,

How to behave will be clear.

 MARY SHARES

Look at the word "BEHAVE."

I see "BE" and "HAVE."

*To "BE" in peace, is to share peace and to share peace is to
"HAVE" peace.*

"BEHAVE" takes on a whole new meaning in your INSPIRED SELF!

"MEET YOUR MENTOR WITHIN"

. . . .

MARY SHARES

We have all had the experience of some thought or idea or awareness come to us as if out of nowhere —

for a moment we feel Truly Moved;

a glimpse of being connected to Something that knows more than our typical mind —

this Something is Inspiration.

YOUR INSPIRED SELF IS THE CONDUIT FOR INSPIRATION.

IT WANTS TO HELP YOU.

COULD YOU USE A MENTOR?

YOU'VE GOT ONE —

IT IS YOUR INSPIRED SELF.

YOUR VERY OWN MENTOR WITHIN.

YOU ALREADY KNOW THE INS AND OUTS OF YOUR EVERYDAY LIFE, RESPONSIBILITIES AND ACTIVITIES.

PAUSE FOR INSPIRATION IS TEACHING YOU HOW TO ENHANCE THE QUALITY OF YOUR EVERYDAY LIFE THROUGH CONNECTING WITH

YOUR MENTOR WITHIN, YOUR GUIDE ON HOW TO MOVE THROUGH THE WORLD.

NOW YOU EXPERIENCE BEING TRULY HELPFUL.

YOU ARE CONTRIBUTING —

YOUR CONTRIBUTION BENEFITS EVERYONE.

IN BENEFITING EVERYONE

IT BENEFITS YOU BECAUSE NOW YOU

EXPERIENCE YOURSELF IN WAYS YOU MAY NOT HAVE EXPERIENCED YOURSELF BEFORE.

A FREE PEACE RISES TO THE SURFACE.

THIS TRANSFORMATION IS SEEING ANEW WITH A NEW VISION OF ONE'S SELF, OTHERS AND THE WORLD.

THE POWER OF THIS NEW VISION IS FAR REACHING.

IT DOES NOT AFFECT YOU ALONE.

IT IS THE **cubicle self mind** HAVING US THINK WE ARE ALONE — SEPARATE FROM INSPIRATION.

THIS IS SIMPLY ANOTHER **cubicle self** MISPERCEPTION.

IT HAS A LOT OF THESE MISPERCEPTIONS BEING THAT IT CANNOT SEE BEYOND THE CUBICLE!

COME TO THINK OF IT, THE **cubicle self** CANNOT EVEN TRULY SEE WHILE IN THE CUBICLE WORLD.

FOR IT RELIES COMPLETELY ON ITSELF TO SEE ANYTHING; THINKING IT IS ALONE, ALL IT CAN SEE IS ITSELF; IT DOES NOT EVEN SEE INSPIRATION

BECAUSE THE **cubicle self** ONLY SEES WHAT IT HAS MADE,

IT IS BLIND TO INSPIRATION —

BUT YOUR WILLINGNESS CHANGES EVERYTHING!

WE ARE ALL IN THIS TOGETHER.

WE COME TO KNOW JUST HOW CONNECTED ALL OF US TRULY ARE IN OUR EXPERIENCE OF INSPIRATION..........

IT IS AN EXPERIENCE WORTH HAVING FOR YOURSELF

TO BE
LIVING
A LIFE
WORTH
LIVING.

INSPIRED SELF QUALITIES

WANT TO HEAR ABOUT THE WONDERFUL QUALITIES OF YOUR INSPIRED SELF?

THE **INSPIRED SELF** IS:

DIRECT AND CLEAR

It is not confused, hence it is not here to confuse; It is not fearful, so it does not cause fear or doubt; It is not a shrinking violet, hence it does not hide its light under a bushel.

Confusion, fear, doubt and hiding all cause

indirect and muddled communication

Your Inspired Self is here to direct the thinking traffic jams

And clear the air. Simply pause.

YOUR INSPIRED SELF IS CREATIVE

It is creative in often unexpected ways — ways beyond your cubicle self.

~~~~~ MARY SHARES ~~~~~

If I had attempted to brainstorm a Truly Helpful program, I would be sharing something my cubicle self thought was helpful; it might have some nice ideas, but upon closer look, I see the cubicle self in its habitual thought pool treading water, efforting to stay afloat. The Inspired Self lets itself be carried along the waves of Inspiration, within the waves of Creativity.

YOUR INSPIRED SELF IS LISTENING

Listening to those thoughts which are worthy of you.

It sees what the cubicle self is going through, but it does not take it seriously or get offended, because It knows that the cubicle self simply doesn't know any better — it is doing the best it can.

Being that your Inspired Self is listening to Inspiration, it is not on the defense; it does NOT jump into your thoughts, the loudest launching a cubicle attack; those loud, overbearing thoughts are coming from the cubicle self's sense of unworthiness.

Your Inspired Self listens to itself and hears the Sound of Peace.

THE INSPIRED SELF NEVER TAKES A DAY OFF

It is available 24/7 in all environments and emotional climates with an infinite amount of energy.

So, you never have to rely on sustaining your cubicle self. When fatigue sets-in and emotions begin taking their toll, that's a sign —

YIELD TO YOUR INSPIRED SELF.

YOUR INSPIRED SELF IS POWERFUL

Its power comes not from having to be in control or controlled, but from being CONNECTED TO INSPIRATION, its power source!

IT IS HELPFUL IN ALL SITUATIONS

No seeming problem is too small or too large for your Inspired Self to dispense Help!

IT IS KEEPING OUR BEST INTERESTS AT HEART

It may not coincide with what we think is in our best interest at the time; It is always something better than we imagined possible. Remember, your Inspired Self knows the big picture.

YOUR INSPIRED SELF IS NOT INTERESTED
IN VALIDATING, BLAMING, SHAMING OR
LAYING GUILT UPON THE cubicle self

Such thinking and behavior is a waste of time and a distraction
from living a life worthy of you. We want to be aware of the cubicle thinking so as not to be led astray into dispiritedness, however,
we need not blame, shame and lay a guilt trip on the cubicle self.

Let Go, LIGHTEN YOUR LOAD . . .
Give all of it to your INSPIRED SELF.

YOUR INSPIRED SELF IS

KEEPING ITS EYE
ON THE GOAL

Shining forth the thought:

I AM HERE ONLY TO BE
TRULY HELPFUL.

YOUR INSPIRED SELF IS INSPIRING

The more we turn towards It the more we want to listen
again and again.

The results and our experience are proof
that being willing, listening to and
following your INSPIRED SELF WORKS,
if PEACE OF MIND IS
WHAT YOU REALLY WANT!

WHAT IS INSPIRATION?

MARY SHARES

We have all been Inspired.

A moment when everything just CLICKS,

The light goes ON . . . YOU KNOW.

WHAT ARE YOU EXPERIENCING IN THESE MOMENTS?

    ENERGIZED

        MOTIVATED

            HAPPY

      FREE

  JOYFUL

INNOVATIVE

    CREATIVE

        A PEACE FLOWS OVER YOU.

THIS IS INSPIRATION WITHIN!

WELL, WHY ARE WE NOT HAVING MORE OF THESE EXPERIENCES?

THEY NEED NOT BE RESERVED FOR SOME SPECIAL TIME AND PLACE.

CERTAINLY THEY ARE NOT BEING RATIONED

BY THE INSPIRATION PATROL.

DO YOU WANT TO BE **INSPIRED?**

TAKE A MOMENT AND ASK THAT QUESTION.

IF YOU GATHER UP EVEN ONE ASPECT OF YOURSELF

THAT YOU HAVE LABELED "GOOD" or "BAD,"

AND PLACE IT UPON THE TABLE OF YOUR

INSPIRING SELF HEART,

YOU WOULD THEN

MAKE ROOM FOR AN

EXPERIENCE OF
INSPIRATION WITHIN.

RELEASING YOUR GRASP ON WHO YOU THINK WE ARE,
WHO YOU HAVE LABELED YOURSELF TO BE,
FOR BETTER OR FOR WORSE,

IS FREEING;

YOU ARE SO MUCH MORE THAN
YOU THINK YOU ARE.

INSPIRATION CANNOT BE DEFINED

AS IT WOULD BE A LIMITED DEFINITION,

AN INCOMPLETE DESCRIPTION.

INSPIRATION IS TO BE EXPERIENCED **IN THE MOMENT.**

SOMETHING WITHIN
SHIFTS,
OPENS,
MOVES

AMIDST THE STILLNESS —

IT IS INDESCRIBABLE;

A GIFT IS BEING OFFERED —

WELCOME IT,

IN THIS MOMENT

INSPIRATION

IS EXPERIENCED

and

You are Present

DO YOU WANT TO EXPERIENCE INSPIRATION?

. . . .

INSPIRATION IS TO BE EXPERIENCED

WE EXPERIENCE IT AS ANOTHER
EXTENDS THEIR INSPIRING SELF TO US.

WE EXPERIENCE IT AS WE EXTEND OUR INSPIRING
SELF TO ANOTHER.

WE CAN EXPERIENCE IT DIRECTLY
THROUGH OUR INSPIRED HEART∞MIND.

INSPIRED SEEING IS
SEEING THAT NOTHING BLOCKS THE FLOW
OF INSPIRATION—

NOTHING!

A PERSON WHO APPEARS UGLY TO US THROUGH OUR SIGHT,
HEARING, SMELLING OR TOUCHING AND JUDGMENT AS WE
PERCEIVE THEM WITH

the cubicle self mind,

WE NOW SEE WITH VISION THROUGH OUR

INSPIRING SELF HEART∞MIND.

JUDGMENTS FALL AWAY

AND WE LITERALLY SEE THEIR INSPIRED SELF.

THE DISPIRITED JUDGMENT OF **the cubicle mind** DISTORTS,

INSPIRATION SEES THROUGH AND BEYOND.

IT IS NOT REQUIRED THAT WE AGREE WITH A PERSON'S BEHAVIOR OR WORDS IN THE WORLD OR ASCRIBE TO THEIR VALUE SYSTEM;

THIS IS NOT THE WORLD OF TRUE INSPIRATION.

IT IS THAT WE ARE WILLING TO SEE THIS PERSON THROUGH AND BEYOND ALL OF THAT INTO HIS OR HER INSPIRING HEART.

NOW THIS PERSON IS BEING SEEN TRULY.

DO YOU NOT WANT TO SEE AND BE SEEN?

HOW WE SEE ANOTHER IS A REFLECTION OF HOW WE SEE OURSELVES.....

THE **cubicle self mind** REVOLTS AGAINST SUCH IDEAS AS THESE;

"Nonsense, nonsense," shouts the **cubicle self**, "i have to judge people to keep my world safe. Not everyone has an INSPIRED SELF, YOU KNOW."

GUESS WHAT?

YES, WE DO.

NOW, NOT EVERYONE IS WILLING TO OPEN THEMSELVES TO INSPIRATION AND ACTUALLY TRUST THIS HELPER!

THAT CUBICLE SELF CAN BE ONE TIGHT CUBICLE!

SO, WHEN THE DARKNESS OF THE CUBICLE CLOSET SEEMS TO BE COMING UPON YOU THROUGH ANOTHER PERSON,

IMMEDIATELY CALL UPON INSPIRATION AND YOUR INSPIRING SELF HEART TO FOCUS ON PEACE.

JUST TELL THE CUBICLE DARKNESS THAT YOU ARE NOT INTERESTED IN WHAT IT'S SELLING AND

FOCUS ON THE PEACE WITHIN YOUR INSPIRING HEART.

Give the cubicle darkness to this Peace.

DIRECT IT TOWARDS LOVE.

WHEN WE ARE WILLING TO EXPERIENCE THE INSPIRED SELF, WE WILL SEE IT EVERYWHERE IN EVERYONE, AND WE WILL THANK EVERYONE TOO, BECAUSE AS WE SEE THE INSPIRED SELF IN ANOTHER,

NOW WE SEE THIS LOVE IN OURSELVES—AGAIN—

BEYOND THAT, WHEN WE SEE THE INSPIRED SELF IN OTHERS, THEY WILL AT SOME POINT IN TIME (MAYBE NOT RIGHT NOW), EXPERIENCE IT IN THEMSELVES!

WHEN?

WHEN THEY LET THEMSELVES BE INSPIRED TO BE TRULY HELPFUL!

THEY MAY CHOOSE TO TURN THEIR BACK ON INSPIRATION AND GO ON **LIVING IN CUBICLE DARKNESS** AND NOT BE INSPIRED TO BE TRULY HELPFUL,

BUT

INSPIRATION IS ALWAYS SHARED
EVEN IF WE ARE NOT AWARE OF IT, EVEN IF WE DO NOT SEE IT –

ALL WE ARE ASKED TO DO IS OUR PART, NOT ANOTHER'S PART!

DON'T EVEN TRY TO DO ANOTHER'S PART —

THAT'S A CUBICLE JOB!

IT IS A **CUBICLE JOB** THAT WILL KEEP YOU FROM DOING YOUR TRUE PART AND KEEP OTHERS FROM DOING THEIR PART—

AND GEE, WOULDN'T YOU KNOW,

THAT IS THE CUBICLE PLAN!!!

IT IS NOT THE WORLD'S RULES AND CONSEQUENCES THAT ARE UP FOR REVISION HERE,

AFTER ALL **the cubicle self** NEEDS A LOT OF RULES AND LAWS AND CONSE-QUENCES, AND SO IT SHALL HAVE THEM IN ITS EXPERIENCE OF ALONENESS IN ITS CUBICLE — SUCH AS IT IS!

THE QUALITIES
OF INSPIRATION

Inspiration carries with it the quality of being still, being alive, being fluid and comforting. It is never doubtful or conceited. Welcome Inspiration with your praise of This Love and listen as Inspiration sings your praises. Inspiration's current flows through tears, laughter, breath, body and soul. Its embrace is sure, its joy everlasting and its creations pure. There is nothing anyone can do to cause Inspiration to stop loving and sharing peace. Inspiration is all that is and will ever be in the Hearts and Minds of those willing to open to its Grace.

OFTEN WE HAVE QUESTIONS ABOUT INSPIRATION.

MARY SHARES

"HOW DO I KNOW THAT WAS INSPIRATION?"

I WILL SHARE MY EXPERIENCE AND YOU REFLECT UPON YOURS.

I EXPERIENCE INSPIRATION AS HAVING MANY QUALITIES:

1) EASE

Inspiration inspires a sense of ease — this does not mean everything we are Inspired to do will be easy; it may be quite challenging and we will come upon obstacles and difficulties, yet like a bird soaring through the trees we can stubbornly crash into the tree forcefully attempting it to move or we can remember "ease" and fly around the tree. What may appear to be a circuitous path is a direct path into Peace.

2) COMFORTING

Inspiration Inspires a feeling of being comforted — comforted in the sense that we feel comfortable. If you feel uncomfortable, there is a reason, and it is an opportunity to look at the discomfort and ask yourself what thoughts and perceptions are causing this discomfort.

Again, following Inspiration isn't necessarily a breeze, there may be some discomfort letting go of cubicle habits, yet something within feels comforted as we choose the guidance of Inspiration —

we know we are on our path to peace.

3) EFFORTLESS

Inspiration Inspires a sense of effortlessness — it is truly amazing, the things we can still accomplish without so much effort. The cubicle self defines itself by how much it produces and pushes. We can meet obligations and be responsible and work productively with patience while leaning into Certainty as our strength.

INSPIRATION IS NOT A PUSHER OR A PULLER!

It doesn't try to push us back into the past or pull us into the future, it simply says, "Be here now." The cubicle self attempts to make the past and future assert themselves in the present to experience a sense of "wholeness" and "completion."

Our completion does not require anything from the past or the future; your wholeness is here now.

INSPIRATION IS EFFORTLESS AND IN BEING SO IS MUCH MORE PRODUCTIVE THAN CUBICLE EFFORTING.

Cubicle efforting is fatiguing because it is all about control.

Inspiration's effortless strength is sustaining because it isn't fighting. This does not mean we don't work — it does mean that we allow Inspiration to work with us.

4) GENTLE STRENGTH

Inspiration Inspires gentle strength; this is the most powerful strength you will ever encounter because it over-minds the cubicle brute strength or bullheadedness. Cubicle strength does not know gentleness, thus it is weak. It is the lightness of gentleness that carries us through the most difficult of times. Letting go is in gentleness.

5) MOVING

Inspiration inspires us to action; we have all experienced a time when we feel Moved to say or do something — to respond as opposed to reacting from anger, fear or guilt. As we respond to this Inspired movement,

we become Inspiration In Motion.

6) STILL

Inspiration Inspires stillness; there are those moments when we are Moved to stillness. Often, we side with cubicle resistance and try to push through this natural pause for the cubicle mind fears stillness. It is in the still point of Inspiration, in the pause, that we come face to face with our Inspired Self.

7) INTEGRATION

Inspiration Inspires a knowing — this knowing happens because we are experiencing integration; we have moved from "understanding" a part of something to experiencing the whole. How does this happen? Through doing; that is, it is one thing to read, study and talk about something, like listening and following Inspiration for example, yet it is the actual practice of listening to and following Inspiration that brings the experience of wholeness and peace. As we practice Being Truly Helpful, we see its value as we experience its value. We experience our value. This experience of wholeness is integration. It may be revealed to us as a peaceful inner knowing that does not require explanation or justification, it simply is, we know it is and that is all that matters ...

it is a matter of the Heart.

INSPIRATION IS UNIVERSAL

The Faces of Inspiration are many, including yours.

No one is without Inspiration for it is with us from our beginning caressing the faces of all, showering its Peace upon them. **In friends and foes, in all kinds, lie the Faces of Inspiration.** The Faces of Inspiration are pure from the inside though perhaps appearing scarred on the outside, or not.

"Be willing to see with Me," says Inspiration, "and I will seek you out so that you may see all there is to see. I see faces blemished, dirty and filled with disgust; I see faces angry, lustful and missing teeth; I see faces filled with sorrow or pretense — yet beyond all of this,

I see you.

You have the power to see
when you choose to see with Me.

MARY SHARES

YOUR INSPIRED SELF-CARE PROGRAM

One night the Faces of Inspiration came into my awareness. Let me share these faces with you; I will begin with a few thought that entered my heart.

Your Inspiring Self Heart and Mind call you to care for them.

What does this mean?

"To care" simply means to "be mindful of, to take heed."

Perhaps you will find it helpful to pause here and contemplate ways that you may be more mindful of your Inspiring Heart and Mind.

Remember,
Inspiration reveals itself to you in many ways.

Yes, though there is only One Spirit of Peace, it is lovely enough to come to us in ways each one of us will understand, identify with and experience — Inspiration will extend itself to us in myriad ways.

INSPIRATION IS UNIVERSAL

What does this mean?

There is nowhere Inspiration will not travel and no willing heart into which it will not enter. It is everywhere. A little willingness to open to its vast Being and there is no problem too small or too large, for it sees all problems as the same; stemming from the belief in aloneness and separation from Inspiration.

What does this mean?

Now, if someone approached most of us on the street and asked if we felt disconnected or connected to the peace of Inspiration, there is a good chance we would say,

"I feel connected."

Yet, if we were to look at the lack of peace that we experience much of the time in our mind, heart, relationships and in the world around us, we are in fact believing in disconnection. You see, lack of peace is not a random event without a cause. It is happening because we are practicing thoughts, perceptions and behaviors that give rise to feelings of disconnectedness; that perpetuate and validate our unconscious belief in separation.

What are feelings of disconnectedness?

Feeling conflicted, angry, irritable, pressured, pain, suffering, sadness ... in other words, a lack of peace.

A lack of peace all brought on by

JUDGMENT!

We can see how judgmental we are as we are willing to look at our thoughts, perceptions and behaviors that are further embedding us in an experience of disconnectedness. These are not random events without a cause; they are migrating around, beneath and through our cubicle mind and are caused by a belief in aloneness and separation.

The cubicle self mind survives on the belief,

"I am alone."

This belief is usually on the outer edges of our noticing or quite a ways beneath the surface. Inspiration is here to replace this belief in separation with an

experience of connection.

If we practice remembering Inspiration over and over again, our problems will take their place in our Inspiring Self Heart and Mind. Problems will be solved because now we will be seeing anew. All the many things in our lives we thought were problems, often fall by the wayside. Or, we may be given a Creative solution that the cubicle self would have never deciphered. Your Inspired Self is the Master of solutions;

sometimes simply by deleting the problem from our mind. **What problem? I thought I had a problem, but it's gone!**

In Peace there are no problems.

And when there appears to be a problem, Inspiration will surely guide you towards its solution and

Companion you every step of the way.

Inspiration is Universal in that it knows you.

What does this mean?

The only way to truly know anything or anyone is not to judge from misperception.

We perceive based on our beliefs; beliefs that may or may not be rooted in the Spirit of Peace and Helpfulness, but cubicle fear!

To judge is to "place meaning upon" based on what we think we know as based in past experiences. This is the difference between judgment based in misperception and perceiving with Inspiration.

Inspiration does not judge you or anyone based on the past or on fear, thus it knows you. Whether you judge yourself as tall, short, fat, skinny, smart, clueless, weak, strong ...

Inspiration sees your judgments and reveals the truth to you about who you really are.

Inspiration extends peace through all forms:

Male, female, infancy, childhood, adolescence, adulthood, older adulthood, health, sickness, work, play, poverty, wealth, single people, married people, divorced people, ethnicity, religion, race, color, animals, trees, flowers, mountains, stones, rocks, oceans, seas, lakes, streams, waterfalls, creeks, planets, sun, moon, stars, and sky.

NOTHING BAFFLES INSPIRATION.

It extends peace constantly in all directions in every way needed by each and every soul.

"NO WILLING MIND WILL BE LEFT UNTURNED BY PEACE."

When I asked my father how he liked his new digs, the Missouri Veterans Home, he said, "Oh, I like it here. There is a prayer for everyone!"

172 : PAUSE FOR INSPIRATION

THE FACES OF INSPIRATION

All right! Now, how might you experience
THE FACES OF INSPIRATION?

The Breath

The Comforter

The Helper Companion

The Teacher

The Mentor Within

The Healer

Indwelling Spirit

ONE ~ THE BREATH

PRACTICE:

Do you ever listen to your breath?

It reflects the Quiet Whisper of Inspiration.

Being present with our natural breathing is calming;
Inspiration is a calm quiet.

Close your eyes and focus on your natural breath now.

Invite Inspiration into your heart and mind; into your
awareness.

Inhale Peace, Exhale Peace.

Let go and receive the Quiet Within.

TWO ~ THE COMFORTER

MARY SHARES

To be comforted is to be assured safety. Inspiration assures your safety.

Safety from what? From the thought that you are alone; it is this thought of aloneness that brings on the experience of feeling unsafe which traps us in fear.

How can we experience this comfort? •

One day I stopped into a nearby monastery to pause for some quiet time. I began with the thought, "Thank you." No sooner did I extend the thought of gratitude,

I heard Inspiration speak back,

"I am thankful for you."

I was floored! Never in my life did I realize that Inspiration Within is thankful for me!

Comfort began to flow.

This Comforter was brought forth to sustain your spirit, yet you sustain the Comforter by allowing The Comforter to comfort.

PRACTICE:

Take a moment now and let your thankful heart go out to this Comforting Spirit and allow yourself to feel how thankful this Comforter is for you.

Giving and receiving mutual gratitude, One–to–One.

THREE ~ THE HELPER COMPANION

Inspiration extends compassion, meaning it has a desire to help. It helps us by walking with us as a Dear Friend and reminding us of true compassion; our desire to love, to be loved and to experience love. Whispering:

Love unceasingly.

Love without measure.

Love without expectation of receiving,

For in your loving all receiving is given you.

I will share Love with you. Now it is yours to share.

Is this not the help we seek?

PRACTICE:

Pause here and ask this Helper for help with a specific situation — appearing large or small.

Trust you and others are receiving the help you need — right now.

FOUR ~ THE TEACHER

Inspiration truly desires to teach you all of its ways of wisdom and loving; for to be wise is to love, and to love is to be wise.

Peace, love, joy are all this teacher has to teach, for this is all it knows.

Be willing to be taught by this Teacher of teachers. To be a student of such is to be a student with great willingness, true desire, vigilance and strong determination to experience Inspiration. Let this Teacher teach you how to live wisely in teaching you love.

BE A GREAT SCHOLAR OF LOVE

Do not depend solely on books for your learning — you may gain information, but you will not discover your Inspired Self — look within to a vast knowledge and find a library of resources. Volumes of the written word, spoken and unspoken lie within.

Your awareness and acceptance of your
Inspiring Heart and Mind is within.

The cubicle heart and mind professes wisdom of the world seeking peace within it. Locked in the parameters of time and space it attempts to limit Inspiration where all things are possible.

It is best not to ignore this cubicle wisecracker, rather, look upon it with Inspiration who will shed light upon its shadows.

What are the cubicle self's motives, desires, intentions, ways of relating and communicating, values, judgments, and past experiences shading your life now?

What is the cubicle self keeping you from?

Go hand in hand with your wise Teacher navigating the twists and turns, back alleyways, main drags and side streets of the cubicle heart and mind. As you look upon these obstacles to peace with your Teacher, Inspiration Within, its wisdom and love will declare you free by showing you your True Nature.

Time and space cannot find their way within your Inspiring Self Heart and Mind, hence not convolute that which is you.

Yours is a path chartered by Love, long before you take it.

All kinds of torment and frivolous distractions appear in the world, yet walk your path anyway, to discover the reality of Peace. All appearances vanish in the presence of the Teacher, who may use a form as if outside of you only so you may learn that this Teacher is truly within.

Here is the value of helping one–to–one.

Here is the value of seeing that we are all customers and extending the best customer service ever to each other.

PRACTICE:

Take a moment now and call upon this Teacher.

Ask this Teacher to reveal Itself to you.

FIVE ~ THE MENTOR WITHIN

MARY SHARES

Believe it or not, you have a personal trainer!

For your Heart and Mind.

A Mentor trains through demonstration; through being that which you long to become. The Mentor Within is passionate about living an Inspiring life. This is how our talk becomes our walk. The Mentor Within is not passive, it is ready to step up to bat, to go from simply being, to

Simply being while doing in the world.

The Mentor Within Inspires passion to live one's Inspiring life "on the outside" as well as on the inside.

Are you Inspired to do your part?

In doing your part, you see the whole.

In seeing the whole, you experience your wholeness.

What is your part? What is your purpose?

The Mentor Within will use your Inspired part to be a demonstration of Inspiration in the world.

Don't think you have an Inspired part?

You are thinking too small.

Inspiration will give you your Inspired part and you will then see beyond the cubicle passions of the world —

Ask for it!

PRACTICE:

Ask your Mentor Within now,
"If I could be Inspired to see beyond my cubicle passions and into my Inspired Purpose, what would you have me see?"

What is important about opening to Inspiration and doing my part?

I am being an instrument of Inspiration.

In doing, I am seeing that I am connected to Something More than me.

Herein lies the peace I seek.

SIX ~ THE HEALER

Inspiration heals dispiritedness.

Imagine, within you is a Healer.

A Healer is one who recognizes the cause of dispiritedness, thus is able to bring true healing by getting to the root.

Inspiration uproots the cause of dispiritedness, the thought of being disconnected, and replants our heart and mind in the soil of connection.

The Healer Within shows us how our thoughts and perceptions are causing us dispiritedness.

PRACTICE:

Notice one dispiriting thought in your mind — a worry, a judgment, an unforgiveness.

Release these thoughts and perceptions that have come into your awareness into the Healer who will reinterpret them for you and teach you something you need to learn. Dispiriting thoughts are remnants of the thoughts of aloneness, unworthiness, guilt and fear.

Do you want to continue to think these dispiriting thoughts? You need not wait upon the Healer Within to immediately show you new thoughts. That may happen or it may not.

Yet be assured that healing is occurring and Inspired thoughts and awareness are available to you. Pause. > > >

PAUSE FOR INSPIRATION

Receive the Healer and the healing within.

Trust healing to be true. Go on about your day. Soon you will notice a lightness in your step, a lifting of your spirit and hope in your heart.

SEVEN ~ THE INDWELLING SPIRIT

MARY SHARES

How is it possible that Inspiration can literally abide in us?

Last I checked, Spirit wasn't classified as an internal organ so that is not how it lives in us. How then?

Spirit abides in you through your

Inspiring Self Heart and Mind.

*Flowing through your Higher Heart —
your Higher Mind.*

What does this mean? What is it that is flowing?

Life itself — the Life beyond what we see and touch everyday.

In our world, life has its ups and downs, but our Life in Spirit is so happy to be alive that as we connect with it, all we can be is incessantly joyful to be alive.

It is in this joy that Life is seen as a Gift.

Life itself is your gift, the greatest gift ever.

No matter what seems to happen in our worldly life, it in no way changes the Gift of Life we have already received in Spirit.

To become aware of this Life, is to be truly alive.

Complaining about the world, plodding through day to day life, making excuses, wishing on a star, planning future happiness, waiting for the weekend

Or for something to happen to make you feel alive, all grow distant the day you realize Your Real Life .

Spirit is the bridge to your Heart and Mind.

Taking you deep within your Self,

Shining forth in your face and seeing through your eyes.

Pause.

Close your eyes and be willing to be present with this Indwelling Peace.

Now, see this Indwelling offer you the

Gift of your Life in Spirit.

MARY SHARES

Listening to the experiences of others who have connected with Inspiration Within is helpful as we are learning how to hear the Guidance of Inspiration Within.

Yet, remember, that to truly learn to discern between cubicle dispiritedness and Inspiration, practice listening for yourself. In deep willingness you will come to recognize Inspiration within your own Heart and Mind. PRACTICE . . .

WHICH DO YOU REALLY WANT?

PAUSE for INSPIRATION

Is about two potential experiences

available to you as you are

in the business of living in the world:

DIS-SPIRITED OR INSPIRED

You move through your day

DIS-SPIRITED OR INSPIRED!

Which do you really want?

Which do you want for your family?

Which do you want for your friends?

Which do you want for the community in which you live?

Which do you want for the world?

Which are you choosing in this moment?

THIS IS THE ONE YOU GET!

THIS IS THE ONE YOUR FAMILY GETS.

THIS IS THE ONE YOUR FRIENDS GET.

THIS IS THE ONE YOUR COMMUNITY YOU LIVE IN GETS.

THIS IS THE ONE THE WORLD GETS!

WHO CARES?

QUESTIONS?

OKAY,

SO NOW THE CUBICLE SELF IS THINKING,

"WHO CARES?"

WHO CARES ABOUT BEING TRULY HELPFUL?
I'VE GOT WORK TO DO.

YOU CARE — IF YOU THINK YOU DON'T CARE
IT IS ONLY BECAUSE

YOU HAVE YET TO MEET

YOUR INSPIRED SELF
WHO
ABSOLUTELY
CARES!!!

"WHAT'S IN IT FOR ME?"

THE CUBICLE SELF QUERIES.

THE ONLY REASON WE ASK THIS QUESTION IS BECAUSE WE FEEL DEPLETED AND WE ARE LOOKING FOR SOMETHING TO FILL US UP.

ONE DAY WE WILL FIND OURSELVES NO LONGER ASKING THIS QUESTION,

"WHAT'S IN IT FOR ME?"

WE WILL BE EXPERIENCING
"WHAT'S IN IT FOR ME"
IN THE MOMENTS OF OUR
BEING TRULY HELPFUL.

"WHO DO YOU THINK YOU ARE?"

THE CUBICLE SELF GOES ON FEELING THREATENED.

HOW WE SEE OURSELVES IS HOW WE SEE OTHERS.

HOW WE SEE OTHERS IS A REFLECTION OF HOW WE SEE OURSELVES.

IN BEING TRULY HELPFUL OUR SELF-IMAGE CHANGES.

IN BEING TRULY HELPFUL THE WAY WE SEE OTHERS CHANGES.

ARE YOU READY?

IT IS NOT THAT WE CHANGE OUR

cubicle self mind
BEHAVIORS TO

be helpful, be kind, be polite, be courteous, be nice ...

YOU GET THE PICTURE

YOU GIVE THE **cubicle thoughts** TO INSPIRATION WITHIN;

NOT FOR REPAIR, TRANSFORMATION, AND RETURN IN SIX WEEKS —

THE INSPIRED MIND IS FAR TOO WISE

TO ATTEMPT TO REHABILITATE **the cubicle mind**

BECAUSE IT KNOWS THAT **the cubicle mind:**

1. Has no interest in being rehabilitated.

2. Likes "makeovers" — never real change.

3. Is only capable of learning **within the cubicle mind.**

EXCUSES, EXCUSES, GOSSIP, GOSSIP

. . . .

"WHO WANTS TO SEE BEYOND THE CUBICLE?"

It is time to bring our Inspired Self out from behind the scenes and into the world. It takes only a moment to make excuses and many moments to clean up the mess.

It takes only a moment to listen to our Inspired Self and Be Truly Helpful.

NO EXCUSES!

DECIDE TO STOP LISTENING TO

the cubicle mind
GOSSIPING ABOUT ITSELF!

WHAT IS GOSSIP?

THE LAZY MIND HARD AT WORK.

WE ARE NOT GOING OUT OF OUR WAY IN BEING TRULY HELPFUL.

WE ARE GETTING OUT OF OUR WAY.

EXCUSES ARE EXHAUSTING — STOP THINKING.

GOSSIPING IS BELITTLING YOUR ALREADY LITTLE SELF!

JUST HOW LITTLE DO YOU WANT TO BE?

IMMEDIATELY GIVE EXCUSES OVER TO YOUR INSPIRED MIND.

SAME FOR GOSSIP!

EVERYDAY OPERATIONS

cubicle self | INSPIRED SELF

cubicle self	INSPIRED SELF
I bolt into the day with my agendas and/or I dread The day with or without an agenda	I move into the day willing to share INSPIRATION WITHIN
I waste time explaining my behavior	I AM WILLING to share INSPIRATION
No one is listening to me	I AM LISTENING
I am sick of hearing myself	I AM INSPIRED
No one receives help	I AM HELPING THE WORLD
I focus on the obstacles "I could, but" "I was going to, but" "But what if?" But, but, but, but, but I have a really big "but"	I see opportunities to experience *INSPIRATION* AND BE TRULY HELPFUL
I exercise regularly by jumping to conclusions	I exercise regularly by stepping Back, stepping aside and letting INSPIRATION GUIDE
I am a puppet of personalities I form my behavior in reaction to another's personality	I LOOK AT ANOTHER AND SEE THE INSPIRED SELF BEYOND THE PERSONALITY
I am Person-"ality" focused	I AM PERSON-REALITY FOCUSED
I take one thought and make up an entire story around it—all fiction	I TAKE THE ONE THOUGHT OF WILLINGNESS, AND LISTEN TO THE WORDS OF INSPIRATION
I am too busy to be inspiring	BEING IN THE MOMENT DOES NOT TAKE UP TIME— IT SAVES TIME

EVERYDAY OPERATIONS

I can't do this 24/7	I AM WILLING IN THIS MOMENT
I am satisfied enough with the THE STATUS QUO WOE	SATISFACTION IS ABSOLUTELY GUARANTEED RIGHT HERE
I make Assumptions and more Assumptions Another reason I have a really big "but"	NO LOOKING BEHIND. HERE I AM IN THIS "NOW" MOMENT.
I am Sleeping on the job	I AM YOUR WAKE UP CALL

WHAT HAVE YOU GOT TO LOSE?

. . . .

THE REALITY IS

EVERYONE HERE HAS ALREADY EXPERIENCED THEIR INSPIRED SELF — A FLEETING MOMENT OF PEACE, JOY, LOVE.

INSPIRATION IS MOVING THROUGH ALL OF US ALWAYS IN ALL WAYS. WE SIMPLY NEED TO NOTICE IT;

JUST AS THE SKY IS PRESENT 24/7, WE JUST HAVE TO LOOK UP!

STILL THINKING?

> "I don't believe everyone has an INSPIRED SELF."

ASK YOURSELF,

WHO IS MAKING THIS STATEMENT,

THE **cubicle self mind** OR THE INSPIRING SELF MIND?

AHA!

THE INSPIRED SELF WILL NEVER MAKE SUCH A LIMITING STATEMENT.

> THE cubicle self mind is constantly questioning itself, feels unsure, and is filled with doubt.

> THE cubicle self mind is suspicious of anything that threatens its cubicle life and it can attack with viciousness to such a threat.

If the **cubicle self** could sing, its range would be suspiciousness to viciousness.

The **cubicle self mind** is endlessly spinning around in its revolving chair

Attempting to understand its own self-made tizzy, while in a tizzy!

No AWARENESS of anything BEYOND THE CUBICLE.

Thus NO AWARENESS OF THE INSPIRING SELF HEART AND MIND.

EVERYONE HAS AN INSPIRED SELF —
LET'S GET TO KNOW IT!

WHAT HAVE YOU GOT TO LOSE???

DISPIRITEDNESS!

That's what!

∞   ∞   ∞

LET INSPIRATION GUIDE

EXAMPLE!

HOW I FOUND YOUBI!

No offense against people with blond hair, but I just didn't care for the fact that my hairdresser had turned my hair from brown to blond! He just couldn't seem to get my brown hair back no matter how many chances I gave him to try. He also didn't really seem to care all that much. Distracted!

Finally, tired of people all commenting on my blonde hair, pros and cons, I asked my INSPIRED SELF to help me find a new hairdresser. That day, I walked into Starbucks for my daily chai and I saw this man who I just had a feeling was a hairdresser. He looked like a man people had described to me as a well known hairdresser in town, but having never met this man I had no idea. As I stood waiting for my chai, I kept getting this nudging inside to just go ask him. "Are you kidding?" I said to my INSPIRED SELF, "I am not that 'kind of person.'" Get this, here I am making judgments about what kind of person would be so forward! Certainly not "my kind" of person. The cubicle self mind loves to classify all of us into various types. This type does this, but would never do that. Another type would do that, but never this. Oh my! Who will I offend next?

I decided I couldn't take my blond hair another minute and I heard my INSPIRING SELF MIND inform me that what is the worst that can happen? So, he's not a hairdresser, you got the wrong guy. Big deal! So, I approached him, "Excuse me, I never do this kind of thing," (I can only imagine what he was thinking), "but, are you a hairdresser?" "Yes, I am," he said with a happy smile. We stood there in Starbucks, him looking and feeling my hair ("oh my, what are people thinking now?" the cubicle self mind, lurking). He explained exactly what he could do to help me and my blond hair. I made an appointment. Voila — the best hair cut and color I have ever received!

PAUSE FOR INSPIRATION

191

Thank You to my INSPIRED SELF.

Now, to some this example may seem lame and even egocentric because how is my hair color going from blonde to brown helping the world?

It isn't exactly what I would call working for a worthy cause.

Yet, it is a worthy cause. It is a worthy cause because I am practicing listening to my INSPIRED SELF who is worthy of my attention in all matters appearing large or small. The issue is not really my hair color!

Ultimately, my hair color is a moot point.

This is an example of Being Truly Helpful simply because I was willing to listen to and follow my INSPIRING SELF HEART. If I can't even trust and follow the inner wisdom of INSPIRATION in the simple things in life, how will I ever trust and follow this Wisdom with those issues that seem more complex? I won't. I will be too afraid and tend to think, "What could my little help do to change the world or help that person?"

TRUST IN OUR INSPIRED SELF IS DEVELOPED BY
LISTENING TO AND FOLLOWING ITS GUIDANCE
IN ALL MATTERS APPEARING LARGE AND SMALL.

Connecting with YOUBI strengthened my trust in the INSPIRED SELF, thus this is helpful to me, and Youbi got a new client which is helpful to him!

BEYOND GOING FROM BLONDE TO BROWN,

I WAS OPENING TO CONNECTING WITH ANOTHER, INSTEAD OF COMING UP WITH EXCUSES OR SOCIAL RULES THAT WOULD KEEP ME FROM CONNECTING AND KEEP ME BELIEVING IN DISCONNECTION!

Plus, as I trust my INSPIRING SELF HEART, this willingness to trust is extended to others without ever having a talk about trust!

I WAS BEING A DEMONSTRATION OF TRUST!

WHEN ONE INSPIRED SELF IS TRUSTED, IT INCREASES EVERYONE'S TRUST IN INSPIRATION!

WHY? Because **BECAUSE WE ARE ALL CONNECTED.**

WHEN WE TRUST THE INSPIRED SELF WE ARE EXTENDING HELP BECAUSE WE ARE DEMONSTRATING TRUST.

AS WE DEMONSTRATE TRUST, OTHERS FEEL INSPIRED TO TRUST THEIR INSPIRED SELF.

THIS IS **THE NATURE OF INSPIRATION —**
IT FLOWS FROM ONE MIND TO THE NEXT.

So, yes, I even get my hair done,
with INSPIRATION leading the way!

TRY IT!

TRY IT WITH GROCERY SHOPPING...

....

MARY SHARES

Ever hear that little voice telling you as you're walking down the paper aisle that you're out of toilet paper and better pick some up, but then the cubicle mind steps in and says, "No, I think I'm not quite out," and so you don't get any toilet paper. Sure enough, you get home and you're in need of toilet paper, and, well then it's just too late . . . isn't it?

IF I AM NOT TRUSTING MY INSPIRED SELF, I CAN BE SURE THAT I AM TRUSTING THE CUBICLE SELF. **WHICH DO I WANT TO STRENGTHEN?**

WE HAVE ALL EXPERIENCED A THOUGHT COMING INTO OUR MIND ABOUT GIVING A FRIEND OR FAMILY MEMBER A CALL OR SHARING A LOVING THOUGHT AND THEN WE MAKE UP SOME REASON AS TO NOT MAKE THE CALL OR NOT SHARE. A THOUGHT TO CONNECT WITH ANOTHER IS COMING FROM YOUR INSPIRED SELF ...

LISTEN AND RESPOND!

WHEN YOU FEEL MOVED TO SAY OR DO SOMETHING FOR ANOTHER THAT WILL DEEPEN CONNECTION, MAYBE IT'S JUST SHARING A LAUGH, SMILE OR HUG,

GO AHEAD.

YOUR INSPIRED SELF IS IN CONSTANT COMMU-NICATION WITH YOU ABOUT EVERYTHING! PAY ATTENTION AND BEGIN SAVING YOURSELF A LOT OF TIME, ENERGY, MONEY AND MISCOMMUNICATION.

BEGIN EXPERIENCING A DEEPER SENSE OF

CONNECTEDNESS.

PAUSE FOR INSPIRATION

MARY SHARES

Stop trying to improve your cubicle self

and appreciate your Inspired Self.

IF cubicle self mind-improvement were the answer,

Don't you think we would be improved by now?

How many gurus does it take

to screw in a light bulb?

None, because the Light is within.

YOUR ACCESS CODE

. . . .

YOUR INSPIRING SELF HEART AND MIND IS NOT
OUTSIDE OF YOU —

IT **IS** YOU.

THE ACCESS CODE IS —

WILLINGNESS

YOUR INSPIRED SELF WILL TRAIN YOU.

IT IS **YOUR MENTOR WITHIN.**

YOU WILL EACH HAVE YOUR OWN EXPERIENCE
OF YOUR INSPIRED SELF,

How to be aware of It and connect in the moment.

AND

THERE IS A SHARED EXPERIENCE
OF THE INSPIRED SELF....

SO, HOW DO YOU
EXPERIENCE
INSPIRATION WITHIN?

OPEN HEART,

WILLING MIND, and

RELEASE PRECONCEIVED NOTIONS.

INSPIRATION FLOWS IN MANY WAYS
THROUGH MANY FORMS.

THOUGH BY NATURE
INSPIRATION IS FORMLESS...

BUT
YOU EXPERIENCE INSPIRATION
AS IT FLOWS THROUGH FORM,

NAMELY YOU.

YOU ARE THE FORM
FOR THE FORMLESS FLOW OF INSPIRATION.

IT IS NOT FORM THAT BLOCKS INSPIRATION

IT IS THE THOUGHT OF
UNWILLINGNESS.

SO MANY TIMES YOU DECIDE AHEAD OF TIME
IN YOUR MIND

WHAT SOMETHING LOOKS LIKE, TASTES LIKE,

IS GOING TO FEEL LIKE OR SOUND LIKE,

ALL BASED ON PAST EXPERIENCE.

REMEMBER,

INSPIRATION
IS HERE **TO SERVE IN THE NOW!**

LET IT SERVE ~

LAB EXPERIMENTS

Here is a story.

LAB EXPERIMENTS

Once in Time...

IMAGINE THE WORLD TO BE A HUGE LABORATORY FOR THE EXPERIMENT OF ARTIFICIAL LIFE.

THE **cubicle self mind** DOES NOT TRULY EXPERIMENT,

IT GAMBLES.

ADDICTED TO THE CYCLE OF WINNING AND LOSING.

It is like a mad scientist in its cubicle laboratory; spilling chemicals, causing explosions, concocting potions with a limited time span.

Eventually the magic wears off and the carriage turns back into a pumpkin and Cinderella has to go back to living with her evil stepsisters.

Waiting again for prince charming to save her from such a lowly existence.

It's back to gambling with its magic.

Woe is me.

...OR...

The cubicle self mind develops the greatest self-defense system known to humankings.

An elaborate formula with a special secret ingredient kept locked in a steel foolproof safe; the safe's code only known by the mad scientist himself and his twin assistant.

The mad scientist sells the "cubicle self-defense system" to the highest bidder in the land in exchange for the assurance of his personal safety and that of his twin.

No sooner did he sell the cubicle defense system did a civil war break out in the land of the highest bidder of which the mad scientist now was a new citizen along with his twin assistant.

What now?

The civil war appears to be between

the northern hemisphere mind and the southern hemisphere mind. You see the cubicle self mind and his twin decided to take a "protected" vacation home in the southern hemisphere,

Lounging under the fiery heat of the sun in an attempt to defrost their cold, cold hearts.

It seems their hearts had become frozen due to lengthy days and nights, year after year after year in the laboratory making the "cubicle self-defense" system.

It turns out the special secret ingredient had a side effect unbeknownst to the mad scientist and his twin assistant.

A side effect I might add, not listed on the package —

a cold heart becoming colder over time eventually leading to

A FROZEN HEART!

Anyway, it turns out that the highest bidder in the land, now sole owner of the cubicle defense system, lived in the northern hemisphere mind and had every intention of finally making use of the cubicle self-defense system on the humankings of his own little kingdom, including the southern hemisphere mind thinkers.

No one was sure what exactly the civil war was about.

The highest bidder in the land apparently kept the cubicle self-defense system close by his side day and night to maintain its safekeeping.

Then one day he came down with a cubicle sickness, an odd flu.

Instead of the typical high temperature we normally see along with other symptoms of the flu,

the highest bidder in the land had a steadily dropping temperature! The doctors were confounded!

No matter how much heat the owner of the cubicle self-defense system was exposed to, his temperature kept dropping.

Medical personnel suggested he move to the southern hemisphere for basking in the heat of the sun.

Of course this was not an option as he had already declared war on the southern hemisphere thinkers; he couldn't switch sides now.

Realizing his death was eminent and not wanting to die alone, the highest bidder in the land crawls to the foolproof safe to obtain his greatest possession.

He enters the foolproof code:

l a m a l o n e

that activates the cubicle self-defense system to destroy the entire world.

Meanwhile, the maker of the cubicle self-defense system and his twin had died for their hearts literally froze to death.

Upon his death bed the highest bidder in the land and owner of the esteemed and sought after cubicle self-defense system, lay there shivering in hopelessness and clothed in layers of despair.

For all of his plans to rule the world had fallen out of his daily planner and into his bedpan

and his platinum watch was running out of time.

Still alive and barely breathing, in the space connecting two breaths, he cries out for help.

A servant comes to his side,

"YES," said the servant,

"HOW MAY I BE TRULY HELPFUL?"

"Who are you?" bellowed the weakened owner of the cubicle self-defense system.

"I AM YOUR GREETER WITHIN," responded the helper.

"I HEARD THE SOUND OF WILLINGNESS; IT IS THE ONLY SOUND I KNOW, SO HERE I AM."

THE GREETER WITHIN STOOD BEFORE HIM CARRYING

A BRILLIANT GLASS DOOR WITH A LIGHT SO BRIGHT

IT BLINDED the sight of the

owner of the cubicle defense system,

who cringed in its PRESENCE.

THOUGH UNABLE TO SEE THE GREETER WITHIN OR THE RADIANT DOOR WITH ITS OWN EYES, the cubicle self mind began gasping for air. Feeling its very existence being threatened, it yelled out haphazardly to no one, **"get that thing out of here, who do you think you are?"** lashing out in its darkness.

"YOU DO NOT REMEMBER ME," SPOKE THE GREETER WITHIN, FOR YOU HAVE BEEN IN A DEEP SLEEP IN the land of the cubicle self mind AND

I LIVE IN THE ENTRANCE OF THE LAND OF INSPIRATION. YET IN THE SPACE BETWEEN IS THE LAND OF WILLINGNESS.

I HEARD WILLINGNESS CALL AND I RESPOND TO EVERY SOUND OF WILLINGNESS.

The access code of

W   I   L   L   I   N   G   N   E   S   S

having been entered,

the Greeter Within opened the Door of Light to the

LAND OF INSPIRATION.

> The man who once believed himself to be owner of the cubicle self defense system now saw himself for the first time.

> "Oh, I am innocent," he whispered gleefully.

INSPIRATION FLOWING FREELY, the cubicle self mind forgot to think about itself.

Without any cubicle thoughts for food it simply began withering away.

> With fits of unwillingness came cubicle thoughts for food,

yet every time the SOUND OF WILLINGNESS

CALLED "IN THE SPACE CONNECTING TWO BREATHS,"

THE GREETER WITHIN APPEARED AND OPENED THE DOOR TO INSPIRATION AND THE INSPIRED SELF.

REMINDING ALL OF THEIR LOVE AND INNOCENCE,

THE INSPIRED SELF IS ETERNALLY SHARING. IN BEING SEEN BY LOVE, IT SEES LOVE AND IS ETERNALLY BEING TRULY HELPFUL.

> ALL THE WHILE, the cubicle self simply ran out of thoughts with which to sustain itself,

> never to exist again.

BEHOLD A LIFE OF INSPIRATION

THE INSPIRING SELF MIND,

INSPIRING TO SERVE LOVE IN THE LAND OF INSPIRATION.

A LOT OF PRACTICE EXPERIMENTING WITH WILLINGNESS IS NEEDED, SO EACH OF YOU MAY ENTER THE LAND OF INSPIRATION.

SO WHERE DOES WILLINGNESS COME FROM?

IT IS RESTING
　　　IN THE SPACE
CONNECTING
　　　TWO BREATHS.

EXPERIMENTS IN WILLINGNESS

. . . .

WHAT IS WILLINGNESS?

Being open to all possibilities

inside this moment.

This moment is not stuck on a clock somewhere.

This moment exists within your Inspiring Self Heart and Mind.

HOW DOES ONE BECOME WILLING?

Simple Question.

Simple Answer.

Simply Say:

"I AM WILLING"
TO INSPIRATION WITHIN.

Now, the walls of the cubicle self heart and
mind are indeed obstacles to experiencing

our INSPIRING SELF HEART AND MIND.

. . . .

IN YOUR WILLINGNESS, INSPIRATION BEGINS TO DISSOLVE THESE WALLS AS MUCH AS WE ARE WILLING.

YOUR INSPIRED SELF OFFERS INSPIRATION TO THE EXTENT THAT YOU ARE WILLING.

SO THERE IS NOTHING TO FEAR.

WE WILL NEVER BE GIVEN MORE INSPIRATION THAN WE CAN HANDLE IN ANY GIVEN MOMENT!

IT IS ALL UP TO US

MOMENT TO MOMENT

MOVING INTO WILLINGNESS

OFTEN WE ARE NOT WILLING BECAUSE WE ARE UNSURE OF HOW OUR

INSPIRING SELF HEART and MIND

MIGHT HAVE US MOVE THROUGH THE WORLD.

THE INSPIRED SELF HAS, IF YOU WILL,

"ALL THE MOVES."

IT WILL COMMUNICATE WITH US IN WAYS WE CAN RECOGNIZE.

OFTEN WE FEEL INSPIRATION MOVING
THROUGH US; A GENTLE PULL, A NOT-SO-GENTLE PUSH
OR A DEEP LONGING AWAITING OUR RESPONSE,

AND THEN,

The cubicle self

Demands our attention.

This is because the cubicle self is a

CREATURE OF HABIT.

Whereas the INSPIRED SELF IS A

CREATION OF INSPIRATION.

As a

CREATURE OF HABIT

the cubicle self heart and mind deplore breaking out of its cubicle and trying something other than a habit!

Dancing around its cubicle, choreographing moves that fit in the cubicle, pushing the limits of the cubicle, climbing the cubicle walls and making up new cubicle dances, some quite complex, vigorous and challenging.

Hours of practice, lots of effort, repetition, repetition, repetition…

Yet never dancing its way out of the cubicle.

We may not be aware of just how much of a

CREATURE OF HABIT

The cubicle self is —

It often is not uncovered until the cubicle self hits one of the walls of the cubicle and gets knocked off its feet and the body goes down with it as well!

Commonly called a

c r i s i s,

due to the Repetitive Motion of the cubicle self;

Thinking the same kinds of thoughts over and over again, making the same judgments over and over again, feeling guilty over and over again, reacting in the same ways over and over again, repeating the same behaviors over and over again, and moving the body in the same ways over and over again.

ITS heart, mind and body ARE VULNERABLE TO REPETITIVE, MULTIPLE INJURIES AND ILLNESSES —

OUCH!

IT IS NOT TO BE BLAMED.

NOR SHALL WE PLACE AN ORIENTAL RUG OVER UNCONSCIOUS' BASEMENT OR

NAIL UP A PIECE OF PANELING OVER SUBCONSCIOUS' CLOSET.

WE CAN LOOK UPON THE CUBICLE SELF

WITH INSPIRATION

AND BE SET FREE!

As a **CREATURE OF HABIT**

The cubicle self simply doesn't know any better
– and it doesn't know any better because this is
simply who it is.

It identifies itself as a cubicle creature of habit.

There it is at a party,

"hi, I'm a cubicle creature of habit."

NOW, THE INSPIRING SELF HEART AND MIND,
AS A

CREATION OF INSPIRATION, HAS ACCESS TO ALL POSSIBILITIES.

THUS IT IS ABLE TO INSPIRE
IN ALL POSSIBLE WAYS.

NO CRISIS HERE!

SEEING THAT THE cubicle self Is limited in its
WORLD OF CUBICLE HABITS,

THE INSPIRED SELF IS WILLING TO BE YOUR
COMPANION IN YOUR EXPERIENCE OF THE CUBICLE,
TEACHING YOU ANOTHER WAY TO BE TRULY HELPFUL.

WITH

JUST A LITTLE WILLINGNESS

RESTING IN THE SPACE CONNECTING TWO BREATHS.

YOUR INSPIRED SELF IS READY
TO DEMONSTRATE THE WAY OUT OF

cubicle thinking!

HEARING THE SOUND OF WILLINGNESS,

INSPIRATION, THROUGH YOUR INSPIRED SELF,

ENTERS THE WORLD OF THE

cubicle self heart and mind —

The cubicle.

INSPIRATION BEING IN THE WORLD,
THOUGH NOT OF THE WORLD, BRINGS
A HEIGHTENED AWARENESS AS IT SEES ALL THERE
TRULY IS TO SEE —

PEACE.

EVEN THOUGH YOU ARE STILL IN THE WORLD AND LOOKING
AROUND YOU SEE CRAZINESS ABOUND,

YOUR INSPIRED SELF IS SEEING
BEYOND THE CUBICLE.

YOUR EXPERIENCES OF SEEING BEYOND THE CUBICLE,
BEING SO REAL,

WILL LEAD YOU TO SEE THAT though we appear to be
IN the cubicle, we are not OF the cubicle

after all...

AND

that it is UTTERLY POSSIBLE to be IN THE cubicle
WHILE BEING IN YOUR INSPIRING HEART
AND MIND!

IT IS NOT ONLY POSSIBLE
IT IS PERFECTLY ACCEPTABLE
AND SOON WE WILL DISCOVER,
A MOST DESIRABLE WAY TO BE IN

the cubicle world.

NOW, BEING A REAL SMART CHAP,

THE INSPIRED SELF IMMEDIATELY SEES
ALL THE WAYS IT CAN COMMUNICATE
INSPIRATION WHILE IN

the cubicle world!

SIMPLY

LOOKING UPON THE WORLD
THROUGH THE EYES OF INSPIRATION,

THINKING THE THOUGHTS OF INSPIRATION,

DANCING IN THE LAND OF INSPIRATION.

"AHH," says the INSPIRED SELF.

SEEING THE body ANEW, NOW, THIS BODY CAN SERVE A TRULY HELPFUL PURPOSE in the cubicle.

THE BODY IS A WAY BY WHICH INSPIRATION MOVES THROUGH **the cubicle,** RATHER THAN BEING A ROBOT FOLLOWING THE ORDERS OF **the cubicle self!**

AHH, NOW I AM INSPIRED AS I INSPIRE!

INSPIRATION IS SO EARTH SHAKING THAT THE BODY, WALKING UPON THE EARTH, IS LITERALLY MOVED INTO ACTION!!!

STILLED IN STILLNESS ~

COMMUNICATING INSPIRING LOVE, INSPIRATION IS NOW SEEN.

INSPIRATION REVEALS IT SELF IN WAYS WE MIGHT NOT HAVE IMAGINED!

IT EXPRESSES ITSELF THROUGH US IN WAYS WE DIDN'T KNOW WERE POSSIBLE ... LET'S GET GROUNDED

INSPIRATION IS NOT SOME FUFU, ETHEREAL, OUT OF SIGHT, ZONED OUT, TRIPPED UP, ARTSY, PSYCHIC, OUTER SPACE, UFO THINGAMAJIGGY........

IT IS ACCESSIBLE TO YOU RIGHT HERE, RIGHT NOW AND IT'S FREE!!!

YOU CAN GET A FULL FREE REFUND IF YOU ARE NOT COMPLETELY SATISFIED.

NO QUESTIONS ASKED.

EXPRESS
YOUR INSPIRED SELF

PAUSE FOR INSPIRATION inspires a way of living in the
world while recognizing that our

True Nature

is Infinite Light

that could never be

OF THIS WORLD.

Though, do not fret.

This most

serene,

still,

always moving,

all embracing

and

Inspiring

Light

serves you well

and everyone else

while we are living in the world.

This Light

enters the world

through

YOU!

YOU ARE A LIVING EXPRESSION OF

INSPIRATION IN THE WORLD.

YES — YOU.

Take a good look at the

cubicle self heart and mind

and all of its various forms of fear.

Take responsibility for

Making it —

Sorry, can't blame anyone any more.

Do not blame, shame or guilt

yourself either.

Simply see the cubicle self thought of disconnectedness for what it is:

Nothing more than a little paper cut.

Take a good look at those thoughts that give rise to a feeling of disconnection from Inspiration, yourself, and others. When they rear their cubicle head again and again, and I assure you they will, you will not mistake them as coming from your True Self.

Give these thoughts over to Inspiration and allow

Peace to

Dissolve your sense of disconnection and dispiritedness and reveal that which is true.

You are a reflection of Love and this reflection is
WHO YOU TRULY ARE —

Eventually

Awareness of Who You Truly Are replaces the belief in

Who You Are Not — the cubicle self

NOW

The scent of purification

comes upon you

NOW

You see, feel and touch

INSPIRATION.

Leading You

Every day in Every way.

Everything

Looks Different

Everything

IS DIFFERENT —

IT IS REAL!

EXPERIENCE YOUR REALNESS —

INSPIRATION HAS ALL THE MOVES

the lightness of a cloud,

the strength of the tide,

the one-pointedness of an arrow,

the everywhereness of the sky,

the swiftness of lightning, and

the lingering of an eagle in flight.

Inspiration is moving through every point in space and all of the space in between —

In time and timelessness.

Inspiration is moving through you...........

Let Your Self Be Moved —

Now!

LOVE

RELATION SHIP SAILING

RELATIONSHIP NUTS & BOLTS

CONCLUSION

RELATION SHIP SAILING

ONE-TO-ONE

Could it be?

Is it true?

Must we, **must we** look at our
relationships?

Do I have to?

Do I have to?

Isn't there some way out of this?

Can't I just make a few phone calls?

Can't I have somebody else examine my relationships
for a small fee?

Can I hire a relationship attorney and have her draw up
some legal papers I can sign?

I'll be in as many relationships as you want, but can somebody
else do the editing—dot the "i's" and cross the "t's?"

NOPE!

There are no little "i's" to be dotted and

No little "t's" to be crossed

Guess Why?

You know already —

Because it is the BIG "I" that we need
look to in our relationships and

the BIG "T" that is the foundation
of our relationships,

so we may Be
Truly Helpful one–to–one!

> It is the little "i" that is the cubicle self, who got
> us into all of our relationships

AND

It is the BIG "I" that is our Inspired Self, who is
going to get us out!

Not out of our relationships mind you,

but the way we perceive relationships and their purpose.

> It is the little "t" of the little "i" that would be
> "cubicle truth," that has misguided all of our
> relationships

AND

It is the BIG "T," our True Inspiring Nature
that is available to Inspire all of our relationships.

BREATHE WILLINGNESS

The Question We Are to Ask of BIG I and BIG T,
about Relationships Is:

WHAT ARE THEY FOR?

Looking at our one-to-one relationships is the key that opens the
lock that opens the door that hits the cubicle wall

> and the cubicle relationship walls
> start tumbling down!

HOLD ON! DON'T START HYPERVENTILATING.

THERE IS PLENTY OF TIME AND SPACE

AND FINALLY

> WITH A WALL KNOCKED DOWN,

SOME FRESH AIR IS COMING IN AND WE CAN,

YES, YES, WE CAN FINALLY BREATHE

Why do we need to breathe?

Remember what happens in the space connecting two breaths?

THE GREETER WITHIN HEARS OUR SOUND OF

WILLINGNESS.

YES, IT'S BACK TO OUR ACCESS CODE.

WELL, IT NEVER REALLY LEFT.

OH, THAT NASTY, SHORT LITTLE CUBICLE ATTENTION SPAN!

You see, the cubicle self has a very short attention span because it is so busy hanging out in the past it simply doesn't have any space left on its hard drive for NOW!

Furthermore, NOW would blow its cover, for it is all about the past!

Even furthermore, the cubicle self is in such a deep state of sleeping and dreaming that it is unaware of the space between the breaths.

Even more furthermore, the cubicle self tends to hold its breath a lot, so instead of a space between the breath it generally finds itself gasping for its next breath — and, well there goes any hope of WILLINGNESS

Right out the window — IF THE CUBICLE HAD A WINDOW!

Luckily, we are fully protected from the tumbling cubicle walls

by our willingness to pause, step back,
step aside
and let Inspiration Guide —

remember?

Have you been practicing
the Inspiring Heart∞Mind Dance?

It is these basic four steps that lay the dance floor
on which

WNYHOO — NOW! can dance.

Nobody dances like our Inspired Self.

One-to-One relationships go from **hazardous collisions**

to

ONE HEART HELPING.

It is not to say that we musn't look upon the cubicle walls
and the cubicle self who made them, for this we are to do.

> Whether we look at them while they are still
> standing, crumbling and tumbling
>
> or after they have completely made their
> downfall,
>
> > that is up to us.

Nevertheless, look upon them we must
AND we musn't stop there,
for we must look upon

> the cubicle mind that built the cubicle, for it is
> the cause of all of our relationship woes.

RIGHT HERE,
RIGHT NOW.

WHERE DO WE BEGIN?

We are in need of no special place, no special time, no special circumstances;

if it is one thing the cubicle self mind has it is

PLENTY OF **CIRCUMSTANCES.**

IT HAS CIRCUMSTANCES AND SITUATIONS AND PROBLEMS AND TECHNICAL DIFFICUL-TIES AND SNAGS AND TEARS AND IFS, AND BUTS

RIGHT UP THE WAZOO!

TALK ABOUT A HEMORRHOID — **OUCH!**

Yes, looking at the cubicle self mind in relation to relationships is quite a HEMORRHOIDAL TASK if you will – pardon the semantics, but we really do have to tell it like it appears to be in order to discover how it REALLY IS!

HOW IT REALLY IS WHEN WE INVITE

OUR INSPIRING HEART∞MIND

INTO OUR RELATIONSHIPS — NOW!

TAKE NOTICE: "NOW" IS ESSENTIAL

IT IS THE WAY THROUGH AND OUT OF
the cubicle self mind

So, we are going to look upon the **cubicle self past**
in the NOW!

We will not be making hash out of the past,

We will not be making stew out of the boo-hoo, but go ahead and
boo-hoo if you need to boo-hoo over the cubicle self boo boo.

We will be calling upon our

Inspiring Self Heart∞Mind

to walk us through the past in this moment.

We will ask our Inspired Self to look upon these situations for us
and use them to bring about peace of mind!

Do not rely on our judgments about the past or our
analysis of the past.

OH MY, OH MY,

WHAT A DEEPER HOLE WE DIG WHEN
WE **LOOK UPON THE PAST WITH THE
SAME MIND THAT CAUSED THE PAST TO
HAPPEN** IN THE FIRST PLACE!

At the time it may appear to be helping us to understand, but
unless we want a true understanding of the how the cubicle self
heart÷mind got us into these messes,

The more messes we will make — of this I am sure!

**Do we really want to anal-eyes the
hemorrhoid?**

WHAT DO YOU THINK?

Let our Inspiring Self Heart and Inspiring Self Mind bring us peace and an understanding that raises us up out of the past, out of the cubicle self and into this very moment where we can begin anew ~

IF WE WANT TO BEGIN ANEW,

WE CAN'T TAKE THE PAST WITH US.

> **THAT IS A BAG YOU CANNOT AFFORD TO CARRY ON!!**

WE DESERVE BETTER.

> AS IT IS IN THE BEGINNING,

> IT IS NOW AND ETERNALLY

NOW.

It doesn't make any difference how right I believe I am about what seemed to happen in the past –

Okay, fine, so I'm "right" — do I feel better?

> NO,

> I just feel right and angry

> or right and sad

> or right and vengeful.

> > **NO ONE EVER FEELS RIGHT AND HAPPY IN THE cubicle mind for any extended period of time.**

> "Right" wears off,

> "Happy" falls away.

MARY SHARES

Someone I knew was in great anguish over a broken relationship. We have all been there.

In talking about the situation and how wrong the other person is,

He kept saying, "BUT what about this," "BUT what about that,"

"BUT I never did that," "BUT I never said that."

Throwing my helpless arms up in the air to INSPIRATION for Help, I heard my Self saying,

"Yeah, the ego has a really big 'BUT'!"

We busted into laughter for how true we knew this to be.

You see, no matter how many witnesses we may round up for our defense, the cubicle self mind does not have a right mind,

It only has a split mind.

Now, you tell me, how can a mind that can never see the whole ever be right?

It can't because a piece of the puzzle is always missing

And that "Peace" is INSPIRATION.

I know it is very difficult to release the past.

The longer we hang onto it, the stickier it gets —

LET IT GO — NOW!

HOW, I HEAR YOU ASKING?

WE MUST DECIDE THAT WE DO NOT WANT RELATIONSHIP UPHEAVEL, BREAKDOWN, FAILURE, NOISE, UPS, DOWNS, CRASHES, BURNS, RUNAWAYS, GETAWAYS, ESCAPADES, GAMES, NIGHTMARES, FACADES, FATIGUE, EXHAUSTION ...

ADD YOUR OWN TO THE LIST

WE MUST DECIDE …

WE HAVE HAD ENOUGH AND THERE MUST BE ANOTHER WAY

AND

WE ARE WILLING TO LET OUR INSPIRING SELF HEART∞MIND SHOW US THE WAY!

IT IS TIME TO WITHDRAW OUR FAITH IN THE
cubicle self heart÷mind

AND

PLACE OUR TRUST IN OUR
INSPIRING SELF HEART∞MIND.

STOP TRUSTING

THE **mind** THAT GAVE YOU
THE HEMORRHOID

TO HEAL THE HEMORRHOID!
IT REALLY IS THIS SIMPLE!

Though the cubicle self heart÷mind prefers to anal-eyes

THERE IS A DIFFERENCE BETWEEN

ANAL-EYES

And

HONESTY

AND IT IS A VERY FINE **CRACK**; I MEAN, LINE.

Analysis is the cubicle self mind looking at something from every angle and considering all the possibilities before making its decision, that is if it ever gets around to making a decision;

Eventually this decision will change or prove to be unsatisfying and will need revision, further analysis — blah, blah, blah.

Honesty is looking upon
the **cubicle self heart÷mind**
with our INPSIRING SELF HEART∞MIND.

Honesty looks right at the turkey and calls it a turkey!

"Yeah George that's a turkey all right, no doubt about it, that's a turkey if I ever did see one!"

Are you harvesting turkey thoughts?

These are thoughts that are stuffing us up and blocking the FLOW OF INSPIRATION ~ ~ ~

Honesty is TRUSTING that our INSPIRED SELF is thinking real thoughts that bring real peace and is WILLING to think these thoughts instead!

TRUE HONESTY in and of its nature will unfold before us the thoughts we are thinking that need to be healed

and these thoughts will be healed as we are willing to have them healed; this is why our analysis is unnecessary.

We don't have to search far — just pay attention.

WHAT ARE YOU THINKING NOW?

WHAT ARE RELATIONSHIPS FOR?

LET US RETURN TO OUR ORIGINAL QUESTION
WITH RELATIONSHIPS.

WHAT ARE RELATIONSHIPS FOR?

All relationships are here to help us Be Truly Helpful.
WHY DO WE NEED TO BE TRULY HELPFUL?

TO COME TO KNOW
OUR INSPIRING SELF HEART∞MIND.

WHY DO WE NEED TO KNOW
OUR INSPIRING SELF HEART∞MIND?

TO EXPERIENCE PEACE.

WHY do we need to EXPERIENCE PEACE?
TO PUT AN END TO PAIN AND SUFFERING OF ALL KINDS.

WHY do we need to PUT AN END TO PAIN and SUFFERING?
TO DISCOVER WHAT IS BENEATH IT.

WHY do we need to DISCOVER WHAT IS BENEATH IT?
BECAUSE WHAT IS BENEATH IT IS YOU!

Yeah, there you are ...
have you been looking for your Self?

Now, if knowing who you are is of no interest to you, that's fine,

GO AHEAD AND CONTINUE LIVING SOMEONE ELSE'S LIFE FOR YOU —

that would be the lie and life of

the cubicle self.

NOW IF KNOWING WHO YOU ARE SOUNDS LIKE A WORTHWHILE IDEA, THEN LOOK UPON YOUR RELATIONSHIPS — ALL RELATIONSHIPS !!!

If you encounter someone anytime anywhere,

this constitutes a relationship!

Length of time spent one-to-one is not a factor in qualifying a relationship as a relationship.

Simply being in the presence of another constitutes a relationship.

We have momentary relationships with passersby, one-day relationships with people we come across in a meeting of some kind, we have week-long relationships while on a retreat, short-term relationships of just a few months, ships-passing-in-the-night relationships that may last a few years, long-term relationships and lifetime relationships.

Ahh, we have more relationships than we ever imagined;

And this is wonderful.

Because now we have unlimited opportunities to come into the awareness of our True Self and Be Truly Helpful!

So, if we forget, don't worry.

We are always given another chance to serve another customer.

READY, WILLING AND ABLE

Throwing a WNYHOO — NOW! event one afternoon, I called the store to order a tray of deli sandwiches. A woman answers the phone, "Deli, may I help you?" "Hi, yes I want to order some sand-wiches for tomorrow. Will that work?" "Uh, yeah I think so," she hesitates. "I'm not really the person who takes the orders, so I don't know. I don't see anybody else around." From the sound of her confusion, I immediately saw the chance for my impatient cubicle self to swing into full gear. Then, I paused. Pausing is so good for bringing up willingness! I saw this as an opportunity to put into practice this whole WNYHOO thing that I would be sharing the next day. Oh, what a novel idea, to practice what I teach!

Willing to be in my Inspired Self, I said, "I really need to place the order now. Do you know what kinds of sandwiches I can order?"

Now, this gave the clerk who thought she couldn't be helpful, the opportunity to be helpful. She responded, "Well, yes, we have roast beef, ham and turkey." "Oh, those all sound great. I need about 75 on dollar rolls." "Okay," as she becomes more willing, "let me write this down. How many of each kind do you want?" "What do think?" I asked, showing trust in her Inspired Self. "Oh, the roast beef is really good, especially with cheddar cheese."

Feeling inspired by her willingness I feel we are on a roll (no pun intended)! "That sounds great," I say, "What other cheese do you have for the ham and turkey?" "Oh, we have cheddar, Swiss, provolone, American. The turkey is good with the Swiss." "Fantas-tic. You are really helping me out, thank you." In a matter of five minutes she had taken my entire order right down to the last detail and we laughed together doing it! I could hear a strength in her voice and a sense of feeling good about herself that she was able to help after all. We both learned.

I discovered the value of pausing and letting my Inspired Self handle a simple practicality and she discovered that she was fully able to do something she had been telling herself she couldn't do! We received our full order; completely intact and delicious.

MEET SALLY AND HERMAN

A FICTICIOUS STORY

"ON THE ELEVATOR"

Sally managed to have locked her keys in the car this morning and with all of the hustle and bustle of breaking and entering into her own car, the entire morning was turning up not as planned!

Having spent several minutes breaking and entering and then even more several minutes explaining to her current boyfriend, Buford, how it was that she attained such abilities, Sally was running quite late for work.

Sally flies frantically through the revolving door into her office, dashing to a big meeting with a big executive who works for a big company who sells big stuff. The more Sally feels rushed, the bigger the company seems to appear in her mind, the bigger the executive looks in her mind with his big face showing a big disapproving grimace for Sally and her tardiness.

Without her usual morning trip to "Uppers Café" for her triple espresso, Sally was beside herself. While she appeared to be running at Olympic speed, she was experiencing her mind immersed in one of those multi-layered jello, sour cream, fruit concoctions and just couldn't seem to find her way out of all of those layers and levels and into the present moment.

Like a fish trapped in sour cream, Sally manages to motion her way onto the elevator.

Out of breath, heavily breathing and mad at herself for being so stupid as to lock her keys in her car, thus not getting her morning liquid lift, "Of all mornings," she lets leap from her lips.

"Of all mornings?" inquires a gentle voice from behind her right shoulder.

"Oh, I'm sorry" says Sally, "I didn't even see you there," explaining herself to a gentlemen holding a tray full of beverages from, guess where? Yes, the "Uppers Café."

"Having a rough morning?" he asks.

"Not compared to the morning I'm about to have without my 'Uppers,' she comments glaring as if dehydrated at his beverage tray.

"Oh, would you like one?" he offers.

"No thanks, I couldn't take your coffee from you. I'm sure someone else needs it," Sally responds while judging herself an idiot for not taking him up on his offer, but it seems rude to accept.

"Well actually, one of these is for you," the gentlemen shares grinning from one side of the elevator to the other.

"For me? How can that be?" Sally wonders.

"Well," he says, "the oddest thing happened at the counter at Uppers this morning. The woman standing in front of me accidentally ordered a triple espresso when she meant to order a double. Uppers being the customer service oriented business that it is, instead of throwing the coffee away or at the customer, the woman didn't want it, so they offered the coffee to me.

I was next in line and the barista looked at me and said, "Need a triple espresso?"

"No, was the first thought that came to my mind because honestly I was already aggravated about having to deal with bringing drinks to the office for my staff. You see, there was a vote to take turns bringing Uppers into the office each morning as a way to be helpful to each other and today was my turn, but I was feeling really put out considering I am, after all, the CEO of the company. Then I heard a thought come into my mind, 'Why Not?' and it leaped from my lips to the barista, 'Why not?'

So, you see, this triple espresso is yours!"

The gentlemen extended the tray of Uppers to Sally, resting his eyes on the triple espresso. Sally gently smiled as she extended her hand to receive what she had so graciously been offered, much to her surprise.

"Thank you so much. By the way, my name is Sally." "Nice to meet you Sally, call me 'H.' You have really brightened my day."

Sally overlooks his brightened day and begins mumbling, "I have this big meeting this morning with this big executive with a really big company and I hope to sell them on some customer service ideas to help improve their business."

The elevator doors open and the two step off the elevator and turned towards one another saying, "Have a good day," only it turns out they are walking in the same direction.

"H" pauses to drop off the coffees to his staff and follows Sally. They are walking into the same boardroom. All the chairs are filled except for one at each end of the table reserved for the two "big executives." Sally looks at Herman, Herman looks at Sally and in their laughing they no longer see "two big executives," rather, their laughter joins them in a feeling of peace. The whole boardroom starts laughing though no one knew what about; the members of each executive's team were simply happy to see their bosses laughing.

Sally and Herman take their seats as equals willing to Be Truly Helpful to one another and their equal companies! As the meeting adjourns and everyone walks out of the boardroom, someone picks up Sally's full coffee cup, saying, "Does this belong to anyone?"

Sally and Herman look at one another and laugh. Sally had been so in the flow of the moment during her presentation, sharing about the giving and receiving of customer service, she forgot to drink her triple espresso that she apparently desperately couldn't function without!

So you see, had Herman not been willing to release his little thought of being "higher on the totem pole" than his employees, he would have never been in Uppers Café.

Had the barista chosen to get ticked off and throw away the triple espresso instead of offering it to Herman, then Herman would not have had the opportunity to listen and follow the direction offered by the thought in his mind of "Why not?"

He would have never been gifted the triple espresso which he then gifted to Sally, which truly lifted her spirits.

Now, Sally is much more open to presenting her sales pitch to Herman. Not because of the triple espresso, but because now Herman has gone from a big executive to an equal partner — a helper.

And in Herman's mind, Sally has gone from a pitch person to an equal partner — a helper.

Now, they and their entire companies are all on the road to Being Truly Helpful.

"LOVE AT FIRST SIGHTING"

A FICTICIOUS STORY

MEET VERONICA & MARVIN

Veronica is new in town and Marvin is "lookin' for love" in all the wrong places! Sound familiar? Yet, even though Marvin has "been there, done that," somehow there was still more "been there, done that" left undone in his meager cubicle perception. Perhaps just one more "been there, done that" and he could say he is done being there and doing that and is finally ready to simply "be" and "do from being."

Veronica makes a grand entrance into "Louie's" dance club with her long, black wavy hair and sculptured eyes and in three seconds Marvin is swept off his feet singing, "I Only Have Eyes For You." Falling into delusions about thinking he is 007 has not served Marvin well thus far in his relationships. The predictable rescuer, lovem' turned victim scenario being his script, Marvin had plenty of practice failing at relationships.

Now, in order to be a rescuer, someone needs to be rescued — here enters Veronica. Veronica was a small town farm girl who had gone to the big city, went to law school and was on the fast track to success. Success defined as money, cars, homes, trips, clothes, a husband and at least one token child thrown in to complete the package!

What is she in need of being rescued from you ask? Good question. Veronica is being victimized by her own little mind telling her what social protocol she must follow to live the life of her planned dreams. Marvin is the perfect rescuer, you see, because his planned dreams of being a wealthy playboy turned devoted husband and father, when he meets Ms. Right, mingle perfectly with Veronica's tale.

WAIT, there's hope. Veronica and Marvin do stand a chance!

Though Veronica and Marvin are clearly delusional, as is everyone during a "Love at First Sighting" episode, they are not as close minded as they appear. For within every mind lies an

INSPIRATION CONNECTION.

THERE IS HOPE FOR EVERYONE!

> Veronica and Marvin began dating thirty seconds into their first dance to some song about being each other's heroes or one and only, you know the song. Six months later they were ushered down the aisle by their loving parents who were thinking behind glass smiles,

"IF THEY ONLY KNEW WHAT THEY WERE GETTING THEMSELVES INTO."

> Seven years later, Veronica would be asking her mother, "Why didn't you say something before the wedding?!"

> Marvin would be asking his father, "What did you do when you couldn't take it anymore?" And now there are the twins, little Jimmy and Josie, who need to be raised amidst the relationship turmoil.

THERAPY SESSION

Seeking help and guidance Veronica and Marvin begin Marital Therapy. Now, Marital Therapy will Be Truly Helpful if the therapist is relying on Inspiration through her Inspiring Self Heart∞Mind to listen and provide therapy. Now, no offense to all of you therapists out there, but I think we can see that no matter what line of work one is in, there is always room for improvement. We can always be more open to Inspiration. Don't worry, all those years of schooling were not a waste of time.

This is the case for everyone. Your Inspired Self will use the tools and skills you learned in school, on your job, in your professional practice, career, spiritual practice and even your intuition, so you may Be Truly Helpful. Inspiration will take your understanding and good intentions and shift your awareness.

It will tilt you from seeing with your **cubicle self mind** to Truly Seeing within your Inspiring Self Mind.

Take everything you have learned from everywhere and bring it to your next class with your Inspired Self!

Are you ready for some postgraduate studies?

Trust inner INSPIRATION and teach others to access and trust this INSPIRATION WITHIN as well.

> Veronica and Marvin's therapist wasn't a bad therapist; she simply was not accessing her Inspired Self Heart∞Mind. It isn't a sin to not be Inspired, it is just the state of the cubicle mind. Veronica and Marvin's therapist was in just that state! But it didn't end there. Listen on.

> Melody, their therapist, who truly was naïve about the cubicle heart÷mind, was of little help to Veronica and Marvin aside from making suggestions as to how to divide up household chores, take turns picking movies, scheduling time for intimacy and quality time and sitting down for dinner with the children at least three times a week. She did provide a safe haven where Veronica and Marvin could share their feelings which helped clear up the bottleneck of emotions clogging their communication so they could at least perform their daily duties. Yet communication was still often taking a detour and winding up at a dead end. What Melody failed to recognize was the fact that Veronica and Marvin were each experiencing

a cubicle self heart÷mind identity crisis which had precipitated the marital discord. They had each forgotten their, yes, you guessed it, their INSPIRING SELF HEART AND INSPIRING SELF MIND!

Their memories of the INSPIRED SELF had faded long, long ago, long before Marvin and Veronica even met. Apparently they had pre-marital counseling, but it seems it made no mention of the Essential Core of a happy life and a happy relationship — BEING AWARE OF ONE'S CONNECTION TO THE INSPIRED SELF! They had covered all of the bases about values, religious beliefs, dreams for the future, family histories, rules of communication, mutual respect ... but, oh my, no sharing of INSPIRA-TION ever occurred!

Off they went after six months of marital coun-seling, somewhat better able to function in the world, for counseling was a safe place to explore, vent and release emotions. They were more organized, assigning chore lists, seeing better movies and having regularly scheduled time together. One thing was still missing —

the realization of the power of their connection to INSPIRATION, as the power Source for a loving, connected relationship.

Unfortunately, as is so often the case, being that the very Source of Life, INSPIRATION, is MIA — Missing in Awareness, their marriage ended six months after the six months spent in marriage counseling. Sorry, no happy new beginning here.

Veronica found someone else seven months down the road to repeat the same cubicle self experiment in hopes of different results — it lasted three months. Marvin went back to

"Louie's," posed at the bar with his eye on the door, looking for another Veronica to walk through it and sweep him off his feet. He found her and got swept right into another cubicle self dustpan and was put out with the cubicle self garbage.

— THREE MONTHS LATER —

Veronica and Marvin meet again at a Pause For Inspiration event-training and begin learning about the treacherous, ignorant and guilt ridden **cubicle self heart÷mind** and the helpful, peace-filled and trustworthy **INSPIRING SELF HEART∞MIND**. And guess who was there? Melody. Yes, she finally admitted she could use a little INSPIRATION herself, and in her therapy practice, being that she wanted to Be Truly Helpful as an Inspired Helper!

Together they learned the access code — remember?

W I L L I N G N E S S

TO BE TRULY HELPFUL

AND DISCOVER WHAT BEING TRULY HELPFUL IS.

NOW, THEY WERE ALL HELPING ONE ANOTHER
IN THE PRACTICE OF
BEING TRULY HELPFUL!

Veronica and Marvin became helpful friends
        to each other
        and more helpful parents to Jimmy and Josie.

Melody began a whole new
        Helping Practice.

NOW EVERYONE HAS TAKEN A MOMENT TO BE
        WILLING TO PRACTICE BEING INSPIRED

AND INSPIRING,
        MOMENT–TO–MOMENT IN INSPIRATION.

CUBICLE GIVING & TAKING

Being Truly Helpful Happens

One-to-One.

We Are All In This Together.

No Matter How Unrelated You May Appear To Be To Another, The Fact Is We Are All Related To One Another In Our Experience of Being Human.

We Share the Air, Water and Space,

But What Really Makes Us All Related Is That

We Share INSPIRATION.

INSPIRATION is like the air as we are all breathing it in all of the time.

INSPIRATION is like the water as it quenches our thirst for fulfillment.

INSPIRATION is like the space in that it is everywhere, always.

THERE IS NO PLACE INSPIRATION IS NOT!

This comes into our awareness as we are willing to

Pay Attention.

THERE IS NO PLACE INSPIRATION IS NOT!

This comes into our awareness when we

share INSPIRATION One–to–One.

Now, this all sounds nice and cozy and all, but I guess you have noticed by now that sharing the air, water and space seems a lot easier than sharing INSPIRATION,

Otherwise, wouldn't we now have more peace-filled relationships?

What happens in the cubicle is that even though we see one another, after all, we're everywhere, it seems we move about as if we are alone;

This is the result of the cubicle mindset.

It is precisely this squared off, locked up and shacked up with nobody mindset that leads us to not even notice that we are not alone, we are actually

IN RELATIONSHIP TO EACH OTHER!

AH, SHOCKING I KNOW!

So, now you know the truth,

We are all related and in relationship.

THIS EXPLAINS
Why Helpfulness Happens One-to-One,

therefore, cannot happen in the cubicle mind-set of aloneness.

So, in every relationship there is One-to-One — a Nut and a Bolt!

Sometimes we're Nuts and

Sometimes we're Bolts!

But one thing is sure,

A Nut is useless without a Bolt

And a Bolt serves no purpose without a Nut!

Much like Giving and Receiving,

They always go together!

Thus, the Nuts and Bolts of every One-to-One Connection is —

Giving and Receiving.

The cubicle self mindset of giving and receiving is "giving" and "taking;" **in every cubicle relationship there is a "giver" and a "taker"!**

Just like the cubicle self to be keeping score while playing solitaire!

HOW IS IT, YOU MAY ASK, THAT GIVING AND RECEIVING ARE ONE IN THE SAME?

Giving and Receiving are One in the Same Because Inspiration springs forth from both Giving and Receiving. Now, being Inspired beings, we already have INSPIRATION to Give; we simply need to be willing to receive what is already ours saying, "Yes, I'll take it." Now in Giving INSPIRATION we receive INSPIRATION yet again

for it is in our giving from INSPIRATION that we realize we have it to give!

This is impossible for the cubicle self to grasp because one hand is frantically and/or reluctantly giving in hopes of getting something in return, otherwise it is just chalked up to more sacrifice; and the other hand is feverishly and/or cautiously taking out of greed based on a sense of lack, and neither hand knows what the other hand is doing so no true giving and receiving is really taking place at all!

Imagine two people agreeing to play toss and one keeps tossing balls and the other keeps catching balls, but the one who is tossing never gets to catch and the one who is catching never gets to toss;

the tosser runs out of balls to toss and

the catcher runs out of balls to catch!

If you see yourself as part of a Giver-Taker relationship, well, it takes two to tango, baby!

What is it that you think you are giving?

What is it that you think you are taking?

Is this an enjoyable game your little cubicle self is playing in your little cubicle heart÷mind or have you worn holes in your socks giving and filled up on an endless supply of nothing taking?

In cubicle giving there is always a point where there is simply nothing left to give — the tank is empty.

In cubicle taking there is always a point where what is being taken has lost its taste — boring!

What usually happens then?

The cubicle self is relentless at seeking and finding new cubicle self playmates.

Cubicle givers generally remain cubicle givers as if branded at birth, and cubicle takers tend to remain cubicle takers as if giving were a four letter word —

What's a cubicle self to do?

"I know," says the cubicle giver, I'll become a cubicle taker! I'll zip up my pockets, sew my arms crossed together and crazy glue my right hand to my left hand — no more giving for me.

NO SIR, I HAVE HAD ENOUGH — IT IS MY TURN! HA! TRY THIS ON FOR SIZE ALL YOU cubicle takers. I'M BRAND NEW BETSY WITH A BRAND NEW TUNE — MY DAYS OF BEING TAKEN ADVANTAGE OF ARE OVER (well, unless you're really nice to me).

NO, I MEAN IT, THAT'S IT, NO MORE GIVING FROM ME, I AM JUST GOING TO SIT BACK AND

TAKE

TAKE **TAKE** TAKE **TAKE** TAKE TAKE **TAKE!**

Now, the cubicle takers are often not so dramatic, unless the givers stop giving and then they might act upset; takers are more sly and clever than that. In fact, they have developed a keen sense of finding the cubicle givers when they least expect it; no one is the victim here, for you see the cubicle givers are happy as clams being the givers until their giving isn't getting them what they had planned for — whether it was the conscious, subconscious or unconscious involved, the cubicle self always has a plan!

Back to the cubicle taker; now these guys generally do not come off immediately as takers; the façade is usually one of temporarily out of luck, self sufficient, frugal savers watching every penny, giving a lot initially to appear as a cubicle giver, then slowly slithering over into the taker category as soon as the cubicle giver is fully on board and giving is pouring in!

A cubicle taker may attempt, but generally only briefly, to change their ways and try their hand at being a cubicle

giver, but having spent their whole life taking, they don't even know how to "pretend give" — and even if they can mimic being a giver, generally their weakness for patience wears off.

> What tends to happen with the cubicle giver "transformed" cubicle taker, is they just can't take it anymore — the lack of "giving" is killing them because after all, that is who they are — givers; they say to themselves, "If I can't start giving to somebody, somewhere, I'll just dry up and die! I think I'll bake a cake — for somebody!" The question remains just what are they truly giving, since with the whole giving process they always seem to find themselves withering away and wind up at a dead end?

What tends to happen with cubicle takers trying on cubicle giving for size is that initially it feels kind of good thinking of someone other than themselves, but after awhile they start wondering,

> "If I'm not thinking of myself, who will be? If I am not around someone who is constantly focusing on taking care of me, how will I survive? Oh my, I better put an end to this before I cease existing!" Here the question remains, if this whole taking thing is such a great idea, how come I never feel satisfied no matter how much I take, no matter how much seems to be given?

Both cubicle givers and takers can be quite charming and appear to be helpful — you see, cubicle givers tend to have a better reputation in the cubicle world than cubicle takers, so it is best to appear as if you are a giver even if you are a taker; however, being that both givers and takers both have a sense of lack and aloneness as their source, there is no qualitative difference between the two.

> Really we could say that the "givers" are just as much "takers" because their giving is

conditional (though maybe appearing uncon-
ditional) and the "takers" can be extravagant
givers all as a means of hiding a deep sense of
insecurity. Cubicle giving and taking stem from
insecurity, being they are rooted in lack — one
cannot give what one does not have and, well,
what is there really to take in nothingness?
Nothingness with conditions and expectations I might add! Maybe in cubicle taking
we may think we are really getting away with
something, but sure enough, if you have been
taking from a cubicle giver, one day there will
be a price to pay!

**You see in cubicle giving and taking nothing is free —
there are always strings attached;**

strings in the form of expectations.

It truly is a wild hunting game of sorts, predator and prey, prey and predator, controller
and controlled, controlled and controller —
the roles of giver and taker are not so cut and
dried, black and white. What is cut and dry is
that underlying both roles is

FEAR

FEAR

And

MORE FEAR!

And then in an effort to not

Feel the fear

We try to pass it off onto somebody else like a
hot potato.

It is like someone let a secret out of the bag and
rather than admitting the mistake, she looks
shocked that anyone would do such a thing
and joins the manhunt to track down who let

the cat out of the bag!!! This evil person must be found and proven

Guilty,

Because she is not going to take the rap for letting loose on the secret for it is just too unbearable to feel all that

Guilt!

But somebody is going to have to feel it!!!

So you see, fear and guilt are at the bottom of this cubicle giving and taking in all relation-ships.

If I just give enough I will not have to feel this fear and guilt;

If I just take enough I will not have to feel this fear and guilt.

Now, feeling guilty about your cubicle giving and taking as well as blaming, being it is all part of the cubicle script, will only perpetuate the mess — instead, just admit your **cubicle giver and/or taker** status and

Ask your Inspirng Self Heart∞Mind to show you another way!

Because one day those **cubicle giver and cubicle taker** walls start needing yet another paint job and well, at some point, the paint fumes become sickening, the paint brushes harden and the paint runs dry!

SOUND FAMILIAR?

DO YOU WANT TO REMAIN IN THE **cubicle world** OF ALL FALSE GIVING AND NEVER REALLY RECEIVING ANYTHING REAL? OR GIVING ANYTHING REAL?

DO YOU WANT TO REMAIN IN THE **cubicle world** OF ALL
TAKING AND NEVER TRULY GIVING ANYTHING WORTHWHILE?

OR RECEIVING ANYTHING WORTHWHILE?

THINK ABOUT IT
for a moment

While you are thinking, ask yourself,

"Who is answering this question, **the cubicle self** or
your Inspired Self?"

The self who needs to be identified and justified
or the Self who is experiencing Peace?

The INSPIRING SELF HEART∞MIND uses the air, water and
space — this would include the body, only for truly useful, worthwhile and meaningful purposes.

The INSPIRING SELF HEART∞MIND makes use of relationships
only for Truly giving and Truly receiving by Being Truly Helpful.

Okay cubicle giver,

"Are you ready to stop singing **'Give You All I Got
Until I Got Nothing Left to Give'** and finding yourself with nothing?"

You too, **cubicle taker**,

"Are you ready to stop singing, **'Taking All I Can Get While I Can
Get It'** and finding yourself with nothing?"

Though these appear as two separate and distinct ways of being in relationship, they are in fact, one in the same;

either path you take, you end up nowhere with
nothing and trying to take it with you!

INSPIRED GIVING and RECEIVING gives you the benefits of both Giving and Receiving.

Two for One — Now, that's an

INSPIRING DEAL!

HOW MUCH ARE YOU WORTH?

No, don't go running to your 401Ks, stocks, bonds, CDs, money markets, real estate, bank accounts — all that.

The question is **not** how much is your

net worth,

The question is

HOW MUCH ARE YOU WORTH?

This is an ESSENTIAL question —

As it is the basis for all genuine Giving and Receiving.

We cannot Give what we are not aware we have and we cannot fully Receive that which we don't even recognize as being worth Receiving!

There is **no genuine giving and receiving in cubicle giving and taking** because **both of these positions**, though appearing oppositional,

are very much the same.

They are the same because both cubicle giving and cubicle taking are motivated by a **sense of lack.**

Where does this gnawing sense of lack, not enough, not good enough **come from?**

Meet

UNWORTHINESS

You've heard of **"Character Defects"**?

> Well, this cubicle character has imagined quite an assortment of these — you've never seen so many fruits and nuts in one cubicle — it's like a fruit and nut factory!

> But his most favorite imaginary character defect and his best friend is

UNWORTHINESS,

Proud child of

FEAR and GUILT,

WHO ARE BOTH DESCENDENTS OF

THE little THOUGHT,

"I AM ALONE."

> The cubicle self mind cherishes **unworthiness** with each fragment of its little mind —

> There just isn't enough the cubicle self can do to support, feed and sustain **unworthiness**.

> To **unworthiness** it owes its everyday existence. If it weren't for **unworthiness** the cubicle self doesn't know where it would be — that is because it would be NOWHERE!

You see, when the cubicle self heart÷mind experienced itself alone in its cubicle, squared off, boxed off and cut off from Life, it

FREAKED

WHERE AM I?

WHO AM I?

WHY AM I?

SUDDENLY IT WAS

N O W H E R E

YIKES!!!!!!!!!

unworthiness came into its little, edgy nowhere mind and promised to keep it company and be its best friend forever —

Finally the cubicle self didn't feel so lonely. It found a "friend," in **unworthiness**.

WHY **unworthiness** YOU ASK,

WHY NOT

WORTHINESS?

I love your questions!

Worthiness

could never be packaged in the assorted fruit and nut basket of the cubicle self heart÷mind — it simply doesn't fit in.

Worthiness is One of a Kind.

Worthiness Fills Every Basket to the Brim With

Thoughts of Inspiration.

There is no room leftover for the

cubicle assortment.

When the cubicle self devised the

Land of Inspiration II, you know, the sequel to the Land of INSPIRATION,

Worthiness was nowhere to be found for Worthiness lives in the

Land of INSPIRATION.

There is nothing like the ORIGINAL

And Worthiness is an ORIGINAL!

unworthiness is a cheap counterfeit, but in our unawareness of Worthiness we think it is all that is available to us. In fact we value it!

So, now ask yourself,

HOW MUCH AM I WORTH?

Cubicle givers and takers are incapable of answering these questions — Cubicle givers generally underestimate their "worth" and cubicle takers tend to overestimate their "worth" —

All the while it is not Worthiness at all they are estimating, but unworthiness, because Worthiness, they simply do not know!

ASK YOUR INSPIRED SELF,

WHAT AM I WORTH?

As soon as you decide to accept your Worthiness, you shall experience

being Worthy.

Your Worth is inestimable, for that which flows from INSPIRATION is not susceptible to less than and greater than.

That which flows from INSPIRATION

is Totally Worthy no matter what!

There is nothing that can be said, done or tried that in any way, shape or form depletes the Worthiness You Are —

Your Worthiness is already done.

Now, only your **willingness** to allow Worthiness to come into your awareness and your simple choice to receive and accept your Worthiness is what will ground you in an everlasting sense of

security, peace and real joy!

It is that simple — really.

Yes, how **complicated** the cubicle self mind wants to make **exchanging unworthiness** for **Worthiness**; for such an exchange is not an even exchange.

This exchange **tosses up the whole cubicle deck of cards** and the game of solitaire, never to be played again.

This exchange **brings security** where once laid insecurity, **peace** where once laid turmoil and **joy** where once laid dismay.

> The cubicle self wants us to think that this exchange is a gamble and we will never get out of it what we put into it —

> Well, it's right about that, because the cubicle self puts in nothing and in return

EVERYTHING

IS

GIVEN,

In Everything Given, Everything is Received.

THIS FREAKS the cubicle self

out because

now it is **nowhere** — again!

Yet, you remain calm as Worthiness is accepted as one's real friend.

This constant Voice of assurance becomes music to your listening.

And what once appealed to you and kept you in chains seems only to be a distant cry of the past, fading, fading and fading evermore leaving no trace of its memory. Now, we can Give and Receive ~

Now, we can Be Truly Helpful

One–to–One ~

"WHAT ARE YOU EXPERIENCING NOW?"

I have been holding off on breaking the news to you, but in order to accept our worthiness, there is something we must come into the awareness of and look at ....

FEELINGS

"Oh NO, not feelings," screams a cubicle perception, "Please don't make me feel. Who is the schiester who came up with feelings anyway?

What good are they? What are they?

Isn't there some way around having to notice what I am feeling? I'm not gonna start boo-hooing if that's what you're up to.

Feelings are just not my cup of tea!"

The reality is, feelings happen!

You have a cup of tea whether you like it or not!

You are having feelings whether you are aware of them or not!

Feelings are driving your decisions, your choices, and your behavior whether you are aware of them or not!

What are feelings?

A feeling is defined as **"a perceived mental sensation."** Now, is that so bad?

"Yes, it's bad. What does that mean anyway?"

Needless to say, the cubicle self is very disturbed (that's a feeling, by the way), about feelings.

"I am not disturbed by feelings," speaks up another **cubicle** perception. "I love to feel my feelings and express my feelings and linger in my feelings and talk about my feelings and vent my feelings and analyze my feelings and let everyone know my feelings. My feelings are my life. I would die without my feelings. **Feelings are everything!!!!!!!!!!**"

Now, these are two extreme cubicle perceptions of feelings; there is also the middle of the road cubicle perception:

Feelings are fine in moderation. Keep feelings in check and don't rock the boat!

What is it about feelings that we either don't want to feel them, we want nothing else but to feel them and make everyone else feel them, too, or we want to wrap them in etiquette?

1. We **fear** being consumed by our feelings.

2. We **fear** losing control.

3. We **fear** feelings taking us to the point of no return.

4. We **fear** being punished for our feelings.

5. We **fear** facing guilt about our feelings.

6. We **fear** we cannot trust our feelings.

7. We **fear** our feelings might be right.

8. We **fear** that my feelings define who I am.

9. We **fear** feeling because we feel all alone.

Notice the theme?

Fear

How do we drop the **fears** around feelings?

Change our perception of feelings.

Feelings are simply perceptions taking on different shapes in response to a thought. Therefore, feelings have valuable information for us as they reflect our thoughts and our beliefs behind those thoughts.

Always look at the thought behind a feeling.

It will tell you what the **cubicle self** is up to which is always **separation, divisiveness, aloneness, disconnection, dispirited-ness**; or the thought will tell you

what the Inspired Self is up to, like peace, joy, love, connection, and being inspired and INSPIRING!

MARY SHARES

We label these various perceptual shapes with words like anger, happiness, sadness, anxiety …

We have perceptions (based on thoughts>based on beliefs) about these labels and then we freak out or feel good accordingly!

What if I asked my Inspired Self to reinterpret my perceptions of anger?

Might I approach my angry feelings differently?

When I feel angry, what if I asked my Inspired Self to show me what I am thinking and give me a healed perception in place of my misperception?

Now, feelings do not need to be feared.
We can welcome the information they bring us.

Since feelings are simply various perceptual shapes, we can be sure that if acknowledged, they will pass quickly, as perceptions are in a constant state of flux.

> > >

When we suppress or repress feelings they become energetically stronger because we are obstructing the flow. As we notice feelings, they flow naturally and balance out on their own.

Our feelings do not own us; we do not own our feelings.

Feelings are helpful. They are knocking at the door of our awareness saying, "Hey, something is up for learning here, something is up for healing here. You might want to pause and take a closer look at me because I have some helpful information for you."

That is all.

Be aware of attempting to "detach" from feelings as this is often misunderstood and shows up as pushing feelings away, repressing feelings, attempting to oppress another's feelings or denial of feelings.

There really is nothing to detach from; rather, there is an underlying misperception to heal. Observe feelings as they are happening, noticing without reacting. In being present to the feeling, the thought behind the feeling may come into awareness.

The feeling – thought combo is moving you into Love or **fear**.

Ask, "Is this feeling – thought coming from **FEAR** or LOVE?"

Be present to fear, with Love, and Love will free you of the fear — this is detachment.

HERE IS ANOTHER TRICKY ARENA!

There are no blanket guidelines about feelings.

You are not being asked to follow a feeling protocol.

Example:

> Anything but a feeling of peace means I am listening to fear, so I better just slam the door on fear's face and wait for peace to show up.

This attitude will never bring real peace.

It is like trying to get a good night's sleep on a lumpy mattress!

LOOK AT THE FEELINGS, ALREADY!

If you feel sad, there is a reason.

If you feel angry, there is a reason.

If you feel anxious, there is a reason.

Until you are willing to look at the reason, you are not opening yourself up to true healing— only temporary **cubicle feel-good** which in fact doesn't really feel good at all; there is still some lump jabbing at your ribs.

The **cubicle self** is smiling ear-to-ear when you are ignoring your feelings because then you are denying yourself healing–peace; peace that you could then share!

HOW DO WE FACE FEELINGS?

Be present with your feelings.

What does this mean?

> Pause.
>
> Be willing to Acknowledge you are having feelings.
>
> Be willing to Call On and come into the awareness of Inspiration Within.
>
> Do not be afraid to Feel the feelings,
> in the Presence of Love.
>
> Notice the thought(s) giving rise to the feelings.
>
> Notice any beliefs about yourself, others and
> the world that are giving rise to the feelings.
> What information do these thoughts have for you?
> Are you holding onto unforgiveness?

Trust Inspiration by being willing to let it go.

This process is

> SIMPLE,
>
> NONJUDGMENTAL,
>
> NONANALYTICAL,
>
> DOES NOT HAVE TO TAKE A LOT OF TIME
> and
>
> IT IS NOT WORK!
>
> > THE CUBICLE SELF WANTS TO
> > MAKE EVERYTHING A JOB.

Allow (*not force*) the feelings to be absorbed into
Inspiration's Peace ~ This happens naturally

~ ~ ~

Also, **practice being present** with Joy, Love and Peace.

Acknowledge their Presence;

These are Your Connections to Inspiration.

How about sensations?

Be present with the sensations.

Pause.

Be willing to **Acknowledge** the sensations.

(a knot in the belly, heart racing or palpitations, tight
shoulders, pain, holding your breath, nervousness …)

Be willing to **Call On** and **come into the
awareness** of **Inspiration Within.**

Do not be afraid to Feel the sensations,
in this Presence of Love, of Peace.

Notice thoughts and beliefs coming up and
the information they are sending you. Are you blaming
yourself or another for something? For the sensation?

Trust Inspiration by being willing to let healing
enter your mind while placing your hands over where on
your body you are experiencing the sensation.

Allow (*not force*) sensations to be absorbed into
the Peace of Inspiration.

A Practice in Accepting Worthiness

THE "P E A R L"

. . . .

PAUSE your mind. Be still on the inside.
Still your body if needed.

EXPRESS your willingness to open to
Inspiration Within; *"I am willing."*

ALLOW Awareness to shift to Inspiration's
Presence within you.

REST with a one-pointed focus on This Presence.
Slow down. Receive.

LISTEN and follow this Wisdom being revealed to you.

STAY AWARE OF BEING CONNECTED

If you become distracted, STAY AWARE OF
BEING CONNECTED by:

Notice you are distracted.

Pause.

Return to your willingness to rest in a
One-Pointed focus on Inspiration Within.

Listen to This Presence of Worthiness
within you. Follow.

PAUSE FOR INSPIRATION

. . . .

273

RELATIONSHIP
NUTS
&
BOLTS

11

. . . .

WAYS

INSPIRATION

INSPIRES

RELATIONSHIPS

RELATIONSHIP NUTS & BOLTS

BEING TRULY "IN-LOVE" WITH EVERYONE

Invitation to Giving and Receiving rather than the games of the "cubicle giver and cubicle taker:" Inspiration speaks, You must let me give to you, before you can give to another. Receiving This Love every day is how you become a vessel of Love in your relationships.

Now instead of never, the past, the future or someday is the "time" to welcome Peace into your relationships. Now is not a hand on a clock. Now is any moment the Hand of Peace gets your attention. Before planning all of your future now moments notice you have arrived in this one. If you are willing to be present in one of your relationships right now, notice how are you being moved to be?

Sanity is the memory of who you truly are. Insanity is the decision to be who you are not. Who you truly are is experiencing joining with others. Who you are not is this "me-character" experiencing divisiveness. You can choose to be the Inspired sane one in this moment.

Peace is the result of moving in the direction of peace. A mind not at peace is a mind practicing conflict. If someone is having a bad day or just a bad personality, do you want to have a bad day too? Peace is a choice. Peace is the patience we all seek in relationships. Practice peace to have peace.

Inner Voice of Love can be taken literally and received through your Inspiring Heart Mind or it can be taken metaphorically and denied. Watch your mind. Have you been talking to your self lately? Which self is doing the talking — your cubicle self or Inspired Self? What is being said? Do you feel cubicle-ized or Inspired? Listen to "not-Love" and you will not love. Listen to Love and you will find your Self, loving.

Rich is the one who stops clothing his mind in rags. What will you think without your raggedy thoughts? What will you talk about without your rags? Who will you be without your rags? Be honest about your rags. See how you value these rags. Are you trying to clean up your relationships with these dirty rags? Turn over your rags to Inspiration Within and allow for a change of mind in your relationships.

Accepting Inspiration Within is the beginning of accepting your Inspiring Heart∞Mind. Instead of trying to change the cubicle heart÷mind into an Inspiring Heart∞Mind, which is never going to happen, accept the cubicle self as it is and open to the True Self in your relationships. Are you willing to accept another's and your True Self?

Trusting in Inspiration Within means that you will stop trying to make the meaningless meaningful. The unconscious cubicle faulty little thought: "I am alone and separate from Love," lays the untrustworthy foundation in cubicle relationships. Harboring this little thought, and you do, is the source of guilt which you now project onto another. The story ends in misery. Be willing to trust that you are connected to Inspiration Within and be taken off of guilt duty. A meaningful, truly trusting relationship is an Inspiration-centered relationship. Do not be fooled by appearances.

Innocence can be received, hated or ignored, but it can never be lost. Innocence is not the opposite of guilt; it is the absence of guilt in the Presence of Inspiration. Allow your own guilt trips to be cleaned up before you pack someone else's bags and send them off on one!

Opportunity is what the Inspired Mind sees; obstacles are what the cubicle mind sees. How do you see? Your biggest obstacle is this "me" character. Your greatest opportunity is this "me" character, when you give it to Inspiration.

Nurturing by our True Nature and the awareness of this Nature is how the cubicle false nature falls away. This is the ultimate challenge of relationships — to bear the letting go of its false nature and trusting that its' True Nature is the real meaning of "In-Love."

TO BE TRANSFORMED OR NOT

In the following "Relationship Nuts & Bolts" section, you will
come to an experiential practice at the end of each section. The
practice of "The PEARL" Inspiring the dispirited, is the foundation
for each of these experiential practices. Within "The PEARL" you
will be guided through a specific practice to help you deepen your
experience of the topic for that particular section. It is your
experience of these 11 Ways that can bring healing to you and
to your relationships.

Suggestion: After reading and being with the material in each of
the 11 Ways, take a few moments to absorb what you have just
read. Each section contains words of Inspired Wisdom, holding the
potential to bring a healing change to your life and relationships.
These simple practices are an invitation to experience the value of
these 11 Relationship Nuts & Bolts for yourself. No one can have
your experience for you. We can read all kinds of books, attend all
kinds of seminars, conferences, workshops, and belong to spiritual
communities, but it is your willingness to open to your experience
of Inspiration Within that transforms. Eventually, we all have to
put our feet to the road.

At the beginning of each guided practice you are guided to Pause.
If you find it difficult to Pause, consider the following ways to
"clear the deck" if you will — to help release surface mental and
physical tension.

- ⊙ Focus on the natural inhalation/exhalation of your breathing

- ⊙ Place one hand on your upper chest; or

- ⊙ Both of the above simutaneously

- ⊙ Take all the time you need. No rush. Inspiration Within is not
    going anywhere. This Healing Presence truly is within.

Your willingness to open to experiencing Being Truly "In-Love,"
helps and heals us all. Thank you.

INVITATION

∙∙∙

INSPIRATION
INSPIRATION
INSPIRATION
INSPIRATION

INVITATION TO GIVING
and RECEIVING

∞

INVITATION INSPIRES
GIVING & RECEIVING

What is Giving but to Give that which You Already Have,
Being that You Received it in INSPIRATION'S Giving to You!

~ INSPIRATION Gives to Us,

We Give INSPIRATION Away,

INSPIRATION comes back to Us,

GIVING AND RECEIVNG ARE

ONE IN THE SAME ~

RELATIONSHIPS are fertile ground for Giving
and Receiving because they are One-to-One.

It is with One-to-One Giving and Receiving
that we experience our connectedness to our Self,

one another

And to INSPIRATION ~

In true Giving and Receiving there is no sense of sacrifice
for we Give from our

INSPIRED SELF HEART∞MIND

who is plentiful and we Receive plenty in return ~

There is nothing more Calming to the Soul,

Loving to the Heart, Mindful of the Spirit

And Peace Bringing to the Body than

Giving and Receiving

From one's INSPIRED SELF ~

Imagine a time when you
Gave from Your INSPIRED SELF —

Maybe it was a smile or the willingness to notice someone's
presence who you might have otherwise ignored, a glance, an
opening of a door, a skip in your step, a cup of grace, a happy
laugh, a gentle touch, pausing long enough to truly see someone,
saying hello to someone you've never met — even a child, looking
into a homeless man's face while giving and seeing the likeness of
your souls ... on and on; Giving with no thoughts of how it might
benefit you, no expectations of ever being paid back, no fear of
sacrifice or interruption to your schedule — Giving and Receiving
are the same and the experience is Pure Joy!

It is not the action that is the True Giving, it is the way in which the action is done, for it is INSPIRED.

INSPIRED ACTIONS ARE MIRACLES!

RELATIONSHIPS ARE OPPORTUNITIES
TO EXTEND AND RECEIVE MIRACLES.

LET NOT ANOTHER DAY GO BY WITHOUT
EXTENDING A MIRACLE!

EVERY MIRACLE YOU EXTEND IS
THE DIFFERENCE YOU MAKE IN THE WORLD ~

LISTEN.

HERE IS A MAJOR POINT:

WE CAN'T GIVE WHAT WE DON'T HAVE!

As I was waking up one morning,
I heard deep in my Inspiring Self Heart∞Mind,

"You must let me give to you, before you can give to them."

Until we are willing to

RECEIVE THE PEACE OF INSPIRATION,
WE TRULY HAVE NOTHING TO GIVE.

We may help out here and there,or you can choose to be an Inspired, Inspiring helper.

> Is your giving wearing you out? Are you build-ing up resentments about being the giver? Have you given and given until you feel you have nothing left to give? Are you asking, "When is it my turn?"

Cubicle giving is the way most of us give.

This is why our giving is so limited.

Clearly, there is no shortage of anything in this world that anyone need be wanting for anything.

> Look around; is this the case?

Why is this the case that so many of us are without basic needs or waiting in our wanting, while not knowing what we really want?

These are the signs of **cubicle giving**!

WHAT IS IT ABOUT OUR TYPICAL WAY OF GIVING THAT SEEMS TO BE CONSTANTLY LACKING,

NEVER ENOUGH?

We Cannot Give What We Do Not Have.

WHAT IS IT THAT I DO NOT HAVE?

The Peace & Love of Inspiration.

WHY IS THIS?

I Have Not Paused for a Moment
To Be Willing to Receive It.

Ask and You Shall Receive.

Oh, it's there waiting for us to receive — there is nothing special we have to accomplish to earn Love or become worthy enough to receive Love — yet we do have to be WILLING to receive This Peace, This Love.

Someday, when you get tired enough, confused enough, doubtful enough or just enough, enough, you will see that even though you may have had good cubicle intentions, you have been either:

> **!** **Giving** from your **cubicle self**.

> OR

> **!!** **Not giving** because **you felt you had nothing** to give.

> OR

> **!!!** **Not giving** because **you were afraid** of running out.

YOU ARE NOT ALONE IN THESE
COMMON CUBICLE GIVING EXPERIENCES!

GOOD NEWS

This Love, This Peace, This Help is ready for you to be willing to receive all of the love and peace and help you will ever need and all of the love and peace and help that you will ever need to give!

MORE GOOD NEWS

Giving happens naturally as you are willing to receive all that Inspiration wants to give you.

THE GIVING BEGINS WHEN YOUR RECEIVING BEGINS.

EXTRA EXTRA READ ALL ABOUT IT

People are reporting that giving is naturally happening in their presence and it is bringing with it great bouts of joy.

We are happy to report that the giving rate is on the increase. People are giving in unthinkable ways without even having planned to do so.

People are giving without even being aware that they are giving,

but a quiet inner peace is

coming over their hearts and

pervading the universe in ways we have never imagined.

Where there was once **suffering**,
now we find contentment.

Where once there was **pain**, now we see hope.

Where **sorrow prevailed**,

Now,

An unexplainable Peace is filling the air ...

HOW DO WE RECEIVE THE PEACE OF INSPIRATION?

Pause regularly.

Say,

"I am willing to receive the

Peace of Inspiration."

Take a quiet moment.

Trust you are receiving.

Remember,

Ask and you shall receive.

Repeat often!

You will be amazed watching the wrinkles in your day getting smoothed out and things that used to be problematic have disappeared.

Watch for the expansion of the desire for peace and the desire to share this peace in your Inspired Heart.

See people smiling at you like they never did before and you smiling like you never did before.

Be a witness to the

simplicity of love.

Be **Truly Helpful** by receiving.

It is in receiving the

Peace of Inspiration

that we Truly have something to give.

IN JOY.

EXPERIENCING
GIVING AND RECEIVING
IN YOUR RELATIONSHIPS

· ·

Pause your mind. Be still on the inside. Still your body
if needed.

Express your willingness to open to Inspiration Within;
"I am willing."

Allow Awareness to shift to Inspiration's Presence within you.

Rest with a One-Pointed focus on This Presence. Slow down.
Receive.

Allow a grievance that you are holding against someone
to come into your mind. Grievances block giving and
receiving.

Observe your thoughts and feelings around this person,
the situation, the relationship and yourself.

Give your thoughts and feelings over to Inspiration's
Presence within you. See your letting go and giving them
over to Peace.

Ask within your Inspiring Heart∞Mind,
"How am I to give, How am I to receive?"

Listen and Follow This Wisdom being revealed to you.

Let go of the outcome.

Give thanks.

You have Accepted Your Invitation to

Giving and Receiving.

NOW

INSPIRATION
INSPIRATION
INSPIRATION
INSPIRATION

NOW

∞

INSPIRATION **INSPIRES** NOW.

NOW IS BEING PRESENT.
BEING PRESENT IS BEING AWARE.
BEING AWARE IS

BEING HERE NOW!

ROLL CALL — ARE YOU HERE?

NOW is the moment to practice GIVING and RECEIVING.

WHERE IS NOW?

NOW IS IN YOUR INSPIRING SELF

HEART∞MIND.

Is it helpful to think about how one could have been more helpful in the past?

Is it helpful to think about how one might be more helpful in the future?

Is it helpful to Be Truly Helpful right NOW?

Lingering in the past or wondering about the future are only helpful to the extent that we are "being present" with such thinking and feeling and being open to Being Truly Helpful now — we can Be Truly Helpful now without regrets for the past or worries for the future —

Being Truly Helpful now heals the past and the future.

∼∼∼∼∼∼∼∼∼ MARY SHARES ∼∼∼∼∼∼∼∼∼

A wise little girl says to her dear mother who is holding herself prisoner to the past and guarding over her future,

"You know, Mom, if you would just be in the present moment, then when the future came around you wouldn't have a past to be so upset about."

HOW TRUE ~

There is nothing that cannot be fully accomplished Now because whatever is happening Now is all that is really being accomplished!

WHAT WOULD HAPPEN IF EACH OF US GOT "CAUGHT UP" WITH LIFE TO BE HERE NOW?

MARY SHARES

If I were caught up on my life I would …

Open a Truly Helpful Center that is free to all and available to everyone all over the world!

Ignore what everyone else says about this idea like that will require a lot of time and energy, you're not capable of running such a center, don't ever work for free people will just take advantage of you … and just do it anyway.

If I ever got caught up with life, I would do everything I am being Inspired to do, but am not doing — NOW ~

Ask Your Self, Your INSPIRED SELF that is,

"If I were 'caught up' on my life, what would I do?"

Who is it that is not "caught up," your **cubicle self** or your Inspired Self?"

IF I WERE WILLING TO BE PRESENT
IN ONE OF MY RELATIONSHIPS RIGHT NOW,
HOW AM I FEELING MOVED TO BE?

NOW, GO BE IT!

Maybe it is simply a prayer — an INSPIRING Thought shared mind to mind.

Maybe that Thought is shared in words or action.

Nevertheless, it is shared because it springs forth from INSPIRATION NOW.

INSPIRATION holds the memory of the Eternal NOW ~

MARY SHARES

I was cooking breakfast one morning and I heard the thought, "Go and extend love to John." "Ah, what a nice thought," I thought, "I will do that later when I finish breakfast."

"Oh really?" queries my Inspired Self.

"Okay, I got It." So, I decide to go find John and dig him out of his office down the hall, and lo and behold, I turn around and there he is, standing right next to me!

He said, "Oh, I changed that light bulb."

> > >

Without a plan for any particular words or behavior, I looked at him, gave him a hug and thanked him for changing the light bulb.

In that **moment**

and for **moments** *thereafter,*

I FELT
MY HEART,
MAYBE FOR
THE ***FIRST TIME!***

EXPERIENCING
BEING HERE NOW

. . . .

Pause your mind. Be still on the inside. Still your body
if needed.

Notice that you are not being present

Express your willingness to open to Inspiration Within;
"I am willing."

Allow Awareness to shift to Inspiration's Presence
within you.

Rest with a One-Pointed focus on This Presence.
Slow down. Receive.

Be Here Now.

Breathe In The Now.

Let The Now Breathe In You.

Listen and Follow This Wisdom being revealed to you.

Let go of the outcome.

Give thanks.

You have Accepted Your Invitation to

Now.

SANITY IS WHAT HAPPENS
WHEN **TWO MINDS** COME TOGETHER
AND REMEMBER **THEY ARE**
ONE INSPIRATION

SANITY

INSPIRATION
INSPIRATION
INSPIRATION
INSPIRATION

SANITY

∞

INSPIRATION INSPIRES SANITY.

SANITY IS WHAT HAPPENS WHEN TWO MINDS COME TOGETHER AND REMEMBER THEY ARE ONE INSPIRATION ~

> Yes, this frightens the **cubicle self mind** for its little solo act is all it has as proof of its existence.

STOP EXISTING,

START LIVING.

DO YOU WANT SANE RELATIONSHIPS

OR

INSANE RELATIONSHIPS?

SANITY IS THE BRINGER OF GOOD NEWS.

SANITY IS SEEING YOURSELF FROM YOUR INSPIRED SELF INSIDE OUT —

FOR IT IS THE INSANITY OF THE **cubicle self**
THAT SEES ITSELF AS A REFLECTION OF THE
INSANITY OF THE EXTERNAL WORLD ~

SANITY IS JOINING
Inspiring Self Heart∞Minds.

INSANITY IS THE STATE OF SEPARATION of cubicle self
heart÷minds.

A SANE relationship reflects the thought of connection ~

AN INSANE relationship reflects
the thought of divisiveness ~

Think about it, when you have a disagreement with someone,
is it really "what" you seem to be disagreeing about that is so
upsetting or is it the disagreeing that is upsetting and the
disagreeing is upsetting because you are experiencing divisiveness
and separation?

Your connection appears to be vulnerable or
broken. ~

{ MARY SHARES

*Mary and John were riding to a meeting together Sunday morning and
Mary decided to please John and take the route he prefers to take, even
though Mary clearly hears within her Inspired Mind not go that way as
for sure there will be a block of some sort.*

Rather than listen and follow Inspiration,

*Mary decides to turn right instead of left, drives about ? mile and,
well, there you have it, sure enough, the road is closed!*

*John laughs and since they are running late says, "Of all mornings
to go this way."*

> > >

Wanting to knock him over the head with the steering wheel if it were only detachable, Mary yellS, "Why didn't you say something if you knew the road was closed?" "I didn't know the road was closed," John laughs, which steams Mary's sight up even more. This is insane, Mary is thinking, "Why didn't I just go the way I heard to go? I am so upset with him!"

The Voice of Inspiration speaks in my mind,

"Mary, what you are really upset about is that you didn't listen to and follow ME.

And in not listening and following the Voice of your INSPIRED SELF, you ended up, literally, at a dead end. Furthermore, and even worse than the closed entry ramp onto the highway, what you are really upset about is how you are allowing this little error to set up a divider wall between you and John.

Your real upset and pain is the sense of separation you are experiencing from another.

MARY SHARES

I find myself admitting this is true. It isn't the inconvenience, being late or having to make a U-turn or even John's laughing that is so upsetting; it is the insane belief in divisiveness; that any little thoughts leading to disagreement or any circumstance could ever have the power to separate what INSPIRATION has joined ~

ALL THE TIME WE THINK WE ARE UPSET OVER SOME HAPPENSTANCE SUCH AS THIS WHEN REALLY, WE ARE NOT UPSET FOR THE REASON WE THINK ~

WE ARE UPSET WHEN WE AGREE ON INSANITY — WE ARE UPSET WHEN WE ARE EXPERIENCING DIVISIVENESS ~

EXPERIENCING
SANITY IN YOUR RELATIONSHIPS

. . . .

Pause your mind. Be still on the inside. Still your body
if needed.

Notice you are experiencing insanity in this moment
Around your thinking about a specific relationship,
activity, circumstance, situation.

Express your willingness to open to Inspiration Within;
"I am willing."

Allow Awareness to shift to Inspiration's Presence
within you.

Rest with a One-Pointed focus on This Presence.
Slow down. Receive.

Ask, "What is the real problem?" Listen.
Ask, "What is the real solution?" Listen.
Decide to Be Willing to Choose the sanity of
Inspiration.
Decide to Be the sane one in this moment.

Listen and Follow This Wisdom being revealed to you.

In Peace is the solution to the disagreement because
In Peace is the solution to the separation experience
Beneath the disagreement.

Let go of the outcome.

Give thanks.

You have Accepted Your Invitation to

Sanity.

PEACE

INSPIRATION
INSPIRATION
INSPIRATION
INSPIRATION

PEACE

∞

INSPIRATION **INSPIRES** PEACE.

WE CAN GO TO PIECES OR HAVE PEACE IN MIND
AS WE ARE WILLING TO GIVE PERCEIVED CONFLICT
OVER TO **INSPIRATION**

IN EXCHANGE FOR P E A C E .

Ah, the Song of PEACE, if only I knew the lyrics. ~

Go through your relationships and assign each one a song — what do ya got?

Country ballads about a good girl gone bad or unreciprocated love, pop tunes about endless love coming to a shocking end, rock songs about sex, betrayal and stolen love, operas of romantic interludes interlaced with murder and intrigue, musicals telling stories of good fortune and happily ever after, heavy metal screaming for an identity, rap tunes rhyming, blues tunes singing the blues, folk tunes talking of life such as it is ...

WHAT ARE THE LYRICS TO YOUR RELATIONSHIPS?

ARE YOU SINGING "HERE COMES THE SUN" OR
"RAINDROPS KEEP FALLING ON MY HEAD"

? ? ?

Your INSPIRING SELF HEART∞MIND is experiencing PEACE in its relationships.

PEACE is standing under the lamppost harmonizing
"SINGING IN THE RAIN"

while the **cubicle self** is busy selling tickets to
"I DID IT MY WAY."

"PRACTICE PEACE TO REMEMBER IT" is
the motto of your INSPIRED SELF HEART∞MIND
in all relationships in every walk of life ~

A person lacking PEACE in life is a mind
not at PEACE ~

**A mind not at Peace is a mind
practicing conflict ~**

A person whose relationships are full of conflict
is a mind feeling conflicted ~

That's Okay —
it is a **common** cubicle experience!

Would you rather be **right** or at PEACE?

> If someone is having a bad day or just a bad personality, do you want to have a bad day too? Do you want to learn conflict along with them?
>
> Do you say to their bad personality,
>
> **"I can be better at being little and pig-headed than you — try this on for size!"**
>
> ## HONK, CRASH, BURN ! ! !

PEACE IS NOT A MYSTERY.

PEACE IS A CHOICE.

PRACTICE CHOOSING PEACE ~

ARE YOU PRACTICING **CONFLICT** OR ARE YOU PRACTICING PEACE?

Being at PEACE may or may not bring PEACE to your relationships; you may witness someone discovering PEACE right before your eyes OR you may witness a person stuck in conflict.

Yet even though you see their cubicle conflict, you are not drawn into the fire with them because you are experiencing PEACE and you are seeing the PEACE within that person instead of the lack of peace he or she is feeling. Your INSPIRED SELF sees the reality of peace behind the façade.

PEACE IS THE PATIENCE WE ALL SEEK IN RELATIONSHIPS ~

EXPERIENCING PEACE
IN YOUR RELATIONSHIPS

Pause your mind. Be still on the inside. Still your body
if needed.

Notice you are not at peace.

Allow something to come into your mind that you want
peace around.

Express your willingness to open to Inspiration Within;
"I am willing."

Feel your lack of peace, whatever it is:
Anger, sadness, aloneness, anxiety, fear,
Worry, confusion, insecurity, doubt, grief…

Allow Awareness to shift to Inspiration's Presence
within you.

Rest with a One-Pointed focus on This Presence.
Slow down. Receive.

Ask, "What thoughts are disturbing my peace?" Listen.
Ask, "How am I sitting in judgment of another or
myself?" Listen.
Ask, "Are these thoughts and judgments Truly Helpful?"
Listen.
Ask, "Is there another way to see this?"

Listen and Follow This Wisdom being revealed to you.

Let go of the outcome.

Give thanks.

You have Accepted Your Invitation to

Peace.

INNER VOICE OF LOVE

INSPIRATION
INSPIRATION
INSPIRATION
INSPIRATION

INNER VOICE OF LOVE

∞

INSPIRATION INSPIRES YOU TO LISTEN TO YOUR INNER VOICE OF LOVE

YOUR INNER VOICE IS THE VOICE OF INSPIRATION AND IT IS COMMUNICATING DIRECTLY TO YOU THROUGH YOUR INSPIRED HEART∞MIND.

LISTEN TO INSPIRATION
EVEN THOUGH THE **CUBICLE SELF** IS NOT.

IT IS THE VOICE THAT IS SPEAKING TO YOU ALWAYS.

HAVE YOU BEEN TALKING TO YOUR SELF LATELY?
WHICH SELF IS DOING THE TALKING?

HAVE YOU BEEN HEARING VOICES?
WHICH VOICE WOULD THAT BE?

YOUR INSPIRED SELF or

The **Cubicle self**

???????????????????????????

What is it that is so important about what the cubicle self is saying that we feel we must listen and hang on to its every little thought?

> And believe these little thoughts.

> And converse with these thoughts.

Would you buy a recording of nonsense, pop it in your player and listen to it all day? Well, that is exactly the way we are spending much of our time!

HOW DOES NONSENSE EVER GET REPLACED BY SENSE?

1) We must recognize the nonsense.

2) We must no longer want to hear the nonsense.

3) We must be willing to let Inspiration remove the **"non"** and give us the SENSE in return.

Is that too much to ask? Who needs **"non"**?

~ WATCH YOUR MIND ~

WHO IS TALKING?

> INSPIRED SELF or **cubicle self**?

WHAT IS IT SAYING?

> INSPIRING THOUGHTS or **cubicle thoughts**?

WHAT IS IT PROPOSING?

TO BE TRULY HELPFUL

or **not**?

HOW DO YOU FEEL?

INSPIRED or **cubicle-ized**?

HOW ARE YOU SEEING YOUR SELF?

WORTHY or **unworthy** of PEACE?

HOW ARE YOU SEEING OTHERS?

WORTHY or **unworthy** of PEACE?

WHAT TIME ZONE IS IT IN?

INSPIRING YOU TO BE HERE NOW

or **ghost of cubicle past or ghost of cubicle future?**

WHAT VOLUME IS IT AT?

INSPIRING GENTLE STRENGTH

or **cubicle concert blaring?**

LISTENING TO YOUR INNER VOICE IS LIKE HAVING A HEART TO HEART VISIT WITH A WISE, LOVING FRIEND.

EXPERIENCING RECEIVING HELP FROM THE
INNER VOICE OF LOVE IN YOUR RELATIONSHIPS

Pause your mind. Be still on the inside. Still your body
if needed.

Express your willingness to open to Inspiration Within;
"I am willing."

> **Notice** you are listening to the cubicle voice.
> **Notice** how it sounds and what kinds of things
> it is saying.
> **Be honest and specific** with yourself about what is
> **Really going on** with your thoughts and feelings.
> **No need to be embarrassed.** This Helper already
> Knows what you are going through.
> This Helper knows you and the **BIGGER PICTURE.**

Allow Awareness to shift to Inspiration's Presence within you.

> **Ask Inspiration Within** to remove from your awareness
> All voices that are not from Love so you may hear the
> Quiet Whisper of Love in your mind.

Rest with a One-Pointed focus on This Presence.
Slow down. Receive.

> **Trust** that Help is here with you now and remains
> with you always.

Listen and Follow This Wisdom being revealed to you.

> **This Wisdom** may be revealed in words, perhaps one
> word at a time.
> **This Wisdom** may be a helpful thought coming into
> your mind.
This Wisdom may come simply as a Silent Presence,
> **A Silent Voice** sharing volumes of Love.

Let go of the outcome.

Give thanks.

You have Accepted Your Invitation to

The Inner Voice of Love.

RAGS TO RICHES

INSPIRATION
INSPIRATION
INSPIRATION
INSPIRATION

RICHES OF INSPIRATION

∞

INSPIRATION INSPIRES
REAL ABUNDANCE.

YOU WILL BE RICH WHEN YOU STOP CLOTHING YOUR MIND IN RAGS.

Have you ever been out at a restaurant and can't help overhearing the people at the table next to you?

Sometimes we need to be an eyewitness to just how much the cubicle self heart÷mind cherishes its raggedy thoughts over the penetrating light of Truly Helpful thoughts, before we can see how much we rely on cubicle thinking and let it run our lives and relationships!

THE **CUBICLE SELF** DOES LUNCH!

The cubicle self loves to "have lunch." This goes far beyond eating — eating becomes an excuse to get together and gripe and complain and gossip and rehash the past and judge and get all worked up over something that happened or didn't happen or something someone did or didn't do or said or didn't say and make plans for how you will treat someone next time you see them ...

This is nonsense and we've all heard it, observed it and participated in it!

How do you feel after such an excursion in the cubicle? Were you able to digest your food? That is, if you ever got around to eating. How do you experience your body — are you relaxed or tense? How is your mind — are you at peace or wound up? Do you feel enlivened with INSPIRATION or dowsed in darkness?

ARE YOU TIRED OF HAVING RAGGEDY THOUGHTS SUCH AS THESE?

Yes, we all have them, but it is time to recognize their lack of value and give them to **INSPIRATION** in exchange for thoughts that are truly valuable ~

No need to deny these cubicle thoughts or "rags" we will call them, for they feel very real to us and appear to be very important and we believe they must be attended to, fertilized and disseminated.

WHAT DO **YOU** DO WITH YOUR RAGS?

COLLECT THEM?

STORE THEM?

SORT THEM?

GIVE THEM AS GIFTS?

Gee, Thanks.

RAGS ARE GENERALLY USED FOR DIRTY JOBS BECAUSE WE DON'T CARE WHAT HAPPENS TO THE RAGS.

ARE **YOU** A DIRTY JOB?

IS YOUR LIFE SUCH A MESS THAT NOW YOU ARE GOING TO CLEAN IT UP WITH RAGS?

DO YOU NOT VALUE YOURSELF ENOUGH TO TRADE IN THE RAGS FOR RICHES?

If **a pile of rags** were placed before you or a calm flow of Peace In Mind came over you and you could choose which you wanted to spend the rest of your life with,

WHICH WOULD YOU CHOOSE?

IT IS THIS CHOICE WE ARE MAKING EVERY MOMENT.

WHERE ARE YOU RESTING YOUR MIND?

When you rest in your Inspired Self Heart,

YOU WILL BE RICH

BECAUSE YOU WILL BE WITHOUT YOUR RAGS!

YOUR RELATIONSHIPS WILL BE RICHER, TOO, FOR YOU WILL NOW BE SHARING REAL ABUNDANCE!

EXPERIENCING YOUR RELATIONSHIPS GOING FROM RAGS TO RICHES.

Pause your mind. Be still on the inside. Still your body if needed.

Stop Ignoring the rags. Rags = the little thoughts of the dispirited cubicle self causing dispiritedness. To be "dispirited" is to be unaware of your True Nature.

Express your willingness to open to Inspiration Within;
"I am willing."

Allow Awareness to shift to Inspiration's Presence within you.

Look at the rags, look at how they are affecting you and Your relationships and the world in which we live.

Be Honest about your rags and who and what you are Ragging about.

Ask, "Are these rags Truly Helpful?"

Do Not Pretend the rags are not there by trying to Cover them up with fresher looking rags.

See how you value the rags and use them as the basis for Your entire life.

Feel the rags. How do you feel holding on to these rags?

Are you willing to discard the rags?

Fear of discarding the rags is a common cubicle phobia! **WHY?**

What will I think without my rags?
Who will I talk to without my rags?
Who will talk to me without their rags?
What will we talk about if we talk without our rags?
What plans will I make without my rags?
Who will I be without my rags?

Rest with a One-Pointed focus on This Presence.
Slow down. Receive.

See yourself giving your pile of rags to Inspiration.
How do you see Inspiration responding to you now?

Listen and Follow This Wisdom being revealed to you.

Let go of the outcome.

Give thanks.

You have Accepted Your Invitation to

True Riches.

Your True Abundance is being present

to your True Nature, Another's True Nature

and the True Nature of the relationship.

ACCEPTING YOUR
INSPIRING SELF HEART∞MIND
IS THE BEGINNING OF EXPERIENCING
A WHOLE NEW YOU.

ACCEPTANCE

INSPIRATION
INSPIRATION
INSPIRATION
INSPIRATION

ACCEPTING
YOUR INSPIRING SELF
HEART∞MIND

∞

INSPIRATION INSPIRES SELF-ACCEPTANCE.

ACCEPTING YOUR INSPIRING SELF HEART∞MIND IS THE
BEGINNING OF EXPERIENCING THE TRUE YOU.

Trying to change the cubicle self heart÷mind is a trying job
indeed — a job that never ends because we are usually trying to
make the **cubicle self** into an INSPIRED SELF,
and well, that just isn't going to happen — ever!

TAKE IT FROM HARRIET!

Harriet attended several cubicle workshops on
self makeovers, changing your life, changing
your kids, changing your husband, changing
your marriage, changing your career, changing
your wardrobe, changing your past ... physical makeovers, emotional makeovers, brain
makeovers and spiritual makeovers. Harriet
was desperate to make herself over; over into
anything other than who she experienced
herself to be. But about two weeks after every
workshop she went from revved up about her
new potential self and life to go along with it
to crashing back down into her old self and the
familiar world of Harriet.

WHY DOES HARRIET KEEP REPEATING THE SAME MISTAKES AND EXPECTING A DIFFERENT OUTCOME?

SHE DOESN'T KNOW SHE IS REPEATING THE SAME MISTAKES —

WHY?

> BECAUSE LITTLE DOES HARRIET KNOW THAT IT IS THE cubicle self mind THAT SIGNED UP, PAID FOR AND ATTENDED ALL OF THESE WORKSHOPS!

I HEAR YOU ASKING,
BUT SHE WAS WILLING TO CHANGE, WASN'T SHE?

> NO, NOT REALLY. YOU SEE, HARRIET WAS WILLING TO CHANGE HER **cubicle self**, WHICH IS NOT REAL CHANGE AT ALL.

> CHANGING THE **cubicle self** IS LIKE CHANGING CLOTHES — THE CHANGES GO OUT OF STYLE, DON'T FIT ANYMORE …!

WE NEED
WILLINGNESS
TO **SEE** OURSELVES **DIFFERENTLY**

AND WE SEE OURSELVES DIFFERENTLY BY
CHOOSING A DIFFERENT HEART,
A DIFFERENT MIND!

BUT WE HAVE TO **GET THE WIZARD OUT FROM BEHIND THE CURTAIN!**

ASKING THE cubicle self mind TO CHANGE US IS LIKE ASSIGNING SOMEONE ELSE THE TASK OF CHANGING YOU – LIKE THE WIZARD!

THEN WE FIND OUT THAT THE WIZARD HAS NO REAL POWER TO DO ANYTHING

EXCEPT MANIPULATE THE CUBICLE!

ARE YOU **WANTING** TO BE **MANIPULATED?**

I THINK NOT!

WHY PUT SOMEONE ELSE, THE WIZARD'S **cubicle self,** IN CHARGE OF YOU?

REMEMBER THE HEMORRHOID?

DOES IT MAKE SENSE TO ASK THE MAKER OF THE HEMORRHOID TO HEAL THE HEMORRHOID?

OF COURSE NOT, FOR IT ONLY HAS THE TOOLS TO MAKE THE HEMORRHOID!

IS THERE A DOCTOR IN THE HOUSE?

YES, YOU!

PHYSICIAN, HEAL THYSELF.

IT IS YOUR

INSPIRING SELF HEART∞MIND

WHO WILL BRING YOU THE TRULY HELPFUL CHANGES YOU SEEK.

The **cubicle self mind** is asleep and dreaming in the land of Oz —

we know what happens there with the Wicked Witch of the West and her entourage —

"I'm gonna get you, my little pretty; and your dog, too!"

I ASSURE YOU, THAT'S A CHANGE YOU DON'T WANT!

THERE IS A CHANGE YOU DO WANT!

A CHANGE OF HEART.

A CHANGE OF MIND.

FROM THE **cubicle self heart÷mind** to YOUR INSPIRING SELF HEART ∞ MIND.

THIS IS THE CHANGE YOU SEEK, BUT HAVE YET TO FIND BECAUSE THE **cubicle self** IS DOING THE SEEKING!

The **cubicle self** will never find your Inspired Self, because **it wants to BE** your Inspired Self. It is seeking to become something that is completely out of its realm.

The **cubicle self** can only be released into INSPIRATION, so that your Inspired Self will then come into your awareness.

Seeking is the means by which the cubicle self attempts to create. It is incapable of creating for it has not the wherewithal to create. Thus, in its dissatisfaction, it is perpetually seeking.

What is the answer? Am I not to seek?

One cannot find something that does not even exist. It appears to exist, but in Inspiration, no cubicle self can be found.

Seek within your Inspired Heart and all seeking will come to an end.

For in your willingness you will reach the end of the **cubicle self**.

Is a little willingness too much to ask when all of Peace awaits you?

WHAT DOES ALL OF THIS HAVE TO DO WITH

RELATIONSHIPS?

Herein lies the downfall of all **cubicle** relationships.

We are seeking for that which does not exist.

We are seeking our Inspired Self in another's **cubicle self**.

The other is seeking their Inspired Self in our **cubicle self**.

Now, if this isn't a cubicle dilemma, I don't know what is!

BACK TO THE LAND OF OZ.

Are you a Wicked Witch of the West?

Are you in relationships with wicked witches?

If we are identifying with the **cubicle self mind, we are ALL the Wicked Witch !!!**

Ugly isn't it?

Even if the Wicked Witch has a makeover, she is still the Wicked Witch !

For her **heart and mind** are living in a dream — a bad dream.

In a bad dream no one is truly helpful; that is what is making it a bad dream.

A bad dream is all about APPEARANCES, so the wicked witch may change her appearance, but it is her heart and mind that are in need of a change ~

318

EXPERIENCING ACCEPTING
YOUR INSPIRING SELF HEART∞MIND

. . . .

Pause your mind. Be still on the inside. Still your body
if needed.

Notice the cubicle self in its seeking.

Where is it leading you?

Express your willingness to open to Inspiration Within;
"I am willing."

Allow Awareness to shift to Inspiration's Presence within you.

Rest with a One-Pointed focus on This Presence.
Slow down. Receive.

Ask, "Who am I?"
Stay Open without preconceived notions and images
of Who you think you are.
Keep Opening to how Inspiration is revealing your
Self to you.
Welcome your Inspiring Self Heart∞Mind into
your awareness.

Listen and Follow This Wisdom being revealed to you.

Let go of the outcome.

Give thanks.

You have Accepted Your Invitation to

Accepting Your

Inspiring Self Heart∞Mind

When you arise each day,
set your mind on your willingness
To Be Truly Helpful for this is welcoming your
Inspiring Heart∞Mind
Into your awareness, your day, your life.
Throughout the day welcome your Self again and again
Simply by whispering "YES" to Inspiration Within.

Do you want to be your Inspired Self in relationships?
In any given moment say in your mind,
"I see my Self being who I am."

As you accept who you truly are,
You are doing your part.
As you do your part,
Others are Inspired to do their part.
You become an agent of Inspired Self-Acceptance.
Each person accepting, being and doing their part.
And so Love flows one–to–one.

TRUST

INSPIRATION
INSPIRATION
INSPIRATION
INSPIRATION

TRUST

∞

INSPIRATION INSPIRES TRUST.

Trust is the **willingness to be aware of Inspiration**, listen to its guidance and follow because you know it will inevitably lead to Peace.

As long as we are feeling guilty and/or seeing guilt in another, there can be no Trust in relationships.

Trust heals guilt.

The **cubicle self mind** version of **trust is very shaky** because it only remains intact as long as someone else is doing life the way we think they should be doing it; so **trust according to the cubicle self is based in**

Behaviors!

The **cubicle self mind** doesn't really care what anyone is thinking, it just **looks to behavior that appears trustworthy.**

This could be called
Superstition.

Superstition is believing that certain behaviors, forms or physical scenarios can call forth specific outcomes —

like breaking a mirror brings 7 years of bad luck!

Or a bride wearing something borrowed, something blue, something old, something new for good luck!

The cubicle self places its trust in superstition — relying on external behaviors and circumstances to bring on a predicted outcome.

APPEARANCES —

to the **cubicle self,** if someone appears similar to us we are more likely to trust; if someone appears different to us, we are more likely not to trust.

the tricky part here is that someone may "appear" similar to us — same values, priorities ... but it turns out that behind closed doors they remove the mask and out comes another appearance.

So, the cubicle self mind is never truly trustworthy or trusting for its trust is based on Appearances

And

Appearances are simply masks.

Masks are meant to hide THE

Lack of trust IN OURSELVES, OTHERS and Inspiration.

cubicle trust is very dependent on whether or not someone meets our standard of behavior.

We may have spent our life trusting someone while they appeared to be doing all the "right" things, **then one day they appear to do a "wrong" thing and we slam down the gavel with a verdict of**

Guilty!

Once **guilt** is decided

Untrustworthiness is not far behind

And **with distrust comes**

Suspiciousness.

Suspicious of any behaviors and/or circumstances that are unlike itself, for in being unlike itself,

The cubicle self feels unsafe.

Being **suspicious**, the **cubicle self must be always**

Defensive — on guard or on the offensive.

Inherent in being on guard or feeling offended is the readiness to

Attack.

So, **what do we have here** in the **cubicle self kitchen?**

Recipe for **cubicle trust**

Have plenty of guilt on hand at all times for this is the main ingredient for all cubicle self mind recipes.

List of ingredients:

Start with **Guilt**

Thicken until you can **cut it with a knife.**

Add a touch of **Superstition** to cut the pain of the guilt.

Put a knife under your cubicle heart.

A dash of **Appearances,**

Ground one **mask of trust.**

A sprinkle of **Suspicion**

Beware of **cubicle spices** that smell different **from you,** for they might come from a bad batch.

Pour in plenty of Defensiveness by putting the knife in your apron pocket as you will be needing it for **Attack!**

Pour all ingredients into a blender and press **"pulverize."**

Pour into little cubicle trays and **freeze.**

Serve separately.

Add **sprinkles of jealousy** or a hint of **niceness** to taste.

There you have it, **Cubicle self trust!**

I wouldn't eat that if you paid me!

But we do, yes we do!

In fact this recipe is the basis for most of our **cubicle** relationships.

And we wonder why our relationships are unfulfilling, unhappy and failing.

WHAT IS TRUST THROUGH THE EYES OF OUR INSPIRING SELF HEART∞MIND?

The INSPIRED SELF clearly recognizes the **cubicle self** and knows the agony of **cubicle trust**, for it is not trust at all. The INSPIRED SELF does not fault the **cubicle self** for It knows that its whole little thought system is based on faulty thinking, being the result of faulty programming, being that it programmed itself.

Hence INSPIRATION is here to Be Truly Helpful — HOW?

INSPIRATION releases the **cubicle self heart** from all of its SECRETS!

Secrets it holds dear in fear.

Which are not really secrets at all because all secrets are built upon the little thought of

"I am alone and separate."

The thought from which the cubicle self was made,

The thought which we are all thinking

consciously, subconsciously or unconsciously.

You see, a **secret** appears to be **a private thought or thoughts that we think**

only we alone know and if anyone were to find out, **we would be FOUND OUT,**

AND **THAT WOULD BE THE END OF THE SELF WE SHOW THE WORLD** AND **LIFE AS WE KNOW IT!**

IN INSPIRATION, THERE ARE NO PRIVATE SECRETS BECAUSE ALL SEEMING SECRETS ARE BUILT UPON

A **CUBICLE** FOUNDATION OF THE **ONE LITTLE THOUGHT** OF

"I AM ALONE AND SEPARATE"

WHICH IS THE COMMON THOUGHT OF THE **CUBICLE SELF.**

WE ARE **ALL** THINKING THE SAME LITTLE COMMON THOUGHT SO IT IS

NO SECRET AT ALL!

THE **LITTLE THOUGHT** COMES FROM THE STRANGE IDEA **WE CAN BE SEPARATE** FROM INSPIRATION!

OBVIOUSLY, THIS IS IMPOSSIBLE.

THOUGH WE MAY APPEAR TO BE SEPARATE, IT IS SIMPLY AN APPEARANCE.

A BELIEF THAT A SUNRAY CAN LIVE SEPARATELY FROM ITS SUN — THAT THE SHINING COMING FORTH FROM A LIGHT COULD SHINE WITHOUT THE LIGHT — IS A BELIEF THAT DEVELOPED FROM THE EXPERIENCE OF ALONENESS AND SEPARATION.

So, INSPIRATION frees us from the

The little thought which frees us from

The cubicle self which frees us from

cubicle trust.

WHAT IS OUR PART?

Giving **the little thought** and all of its successors to INSPIRATION for Release.

> You see, when we think we are keeping secrets or that another is keeping secrets, there can only be **cubicle trust** or REALLY **distrust**.

> However, when we see that **any seeming secrets that the cubicle self may keep are meaningless** because they are **from the meaningless little thought** that we can be separate from INSPIRATION,

we become aware of the MEANINGFUL in the place of the meaninglessness —

And it is upon THE MEANINGFUL that REAL TRUST IS CULTIVATED and EXPERIENCED.

Meaninglessness is inherently lacking in trust for it is lacking in meaning.

When we see the MEANINGFUL,
we automatically trust because It resonates within us
as real.

NOW, we are getting somewhere.

We are getting to the heart of One–to–One
Truly Helpful Relationships

TRUST THE MEANINGFUL.

All True Help Rests on the MEANINGFUL.

No one is seeking **meaningless help** — right?

We are seeking MEANINGFUL HELP;

Help that brings about a change in how we see
ourselves and one another —

A way of seeing that brings Peace in Heart and Mind.

THE RECIPE FOR EXPERIENCING TRUSTING THE MEANINGFUL

Pause your mind. Be still on the inside. Still your body
if needed.

Express your willingness to open to Inspiration Within;
"*I am willing.*"

Have plenty of **Willingness** on hand to be used
little by little, moment to moment, as it is the basis for
the meaninglessness to be seen for what it is and be
released so your hands are Free to receive the
Meaningful.

Allow Awareness to shift to Inspiration's Presence within you.

Give your "secrets" the thoughts, memories and
experiences That you have been holding back from
releasing, over to Inspiration Within, the Bringer
of Meaning.

Be Patient as the cubicle self is a vanishing breed, but
it does not give up without a fight.

The Bringer of Meaning mixes your willingness,
your secrets And the little thought of aloneness until all
is completely Dissolved, including the guilt.

Rest with a One-Pointed focus on This Presence.
Slow down. Receive.

Let the Meaningful Rise in Stillness in place of the
meaninglessness. Be present with Its rising.

See your trusting the Meaningful.

Listen and Follow This Wisdom being revealed to you.

Serve the Meaningful to all.

Let go of the outcome.

Give thanks.

You have Accepted Your Invitation to

Trust.

P.S. This is not the "trust" we may have learned

growing up in the cubicle.

It is the Trust that sets the table for the Feast of Love —

a Feast of Meaningfulness

that we can experience in the world,

though This Love is not of the world.

It is the Trust that we must come to experience

if we are to Be Truly Helpful.

INNOCENCE

INSPIRATION

INSPIRATION

INSPIRATION

INSPIRATION

INNOCENCE

∞

INSPIRATION INSPIRES INNOCENCE.

Innocence is the Heart of Inspiration.

Our willingness to be present within our Inspiring Heart is our willingness to experience our Innocence.

If we are not innocent, what are we?

GUILTY!

It is difficult, in fact impossible, to feel our innocence within the cubicle self heart because of all of the guilty baggage packed in the cubicle.

The cubicle self has packed enough guilt for the trip of a lifetime.

The cubicle self would not recognize innocence if it walked in front of it and caused the cubicle grocery bag mind to spill all of its contents.

After all, there is still the bag, eagerly waiting to be filled by still more of the cubicle self fulfillment and guilt preached by the cubicle world.

The whole cubicle mind must be relinquished to Inspiration, bag and guilty contents!

ARE YOU **GUILTY**?

DID YOU GET A "YES" AND "NO" RESPONSE TO THAT QUESTION?

> Even if you said "no" to yourself, was there a little twinge of a guilt feeling in there some-where?

Well, there you have it!

> Can you be **guilty** and innocent?

How would **that** work?

This is what the cubicle heart tries to pull over on us — it will tell us either that we are as **"guilty as sin,"** or **"I have done nothing to feel guilty about."** It doesn't usually speak of innocence.

> It speaks of **"guilty"** or **"not guilty."**

> No one in a court of law, and **the cubicle heart÷mind is like a court of law**, is ever put on trial and found, "INNOCENT." Rather they are declared **"Not Guilty."** Never will the cubicle heart experience innocence. Why? Because it has declared itself, **"Guilty."** Guilty of what? **Guilty of not being inno-cent!** Why is it not innocent?

Because it has turned away from where innocence lies, in the Heart of Inspiration.

So, you think you don't feel **guilty** about anything?

Ha!

~~~~~~~~~~~~~~~~~ MARY SHARES ~~~~~~~~~~~~~~~~~

I used to walk around with such naïvete. The cubicle heart is gullible and quite sophisticated in hiding guilt. One day I decided to sit down and go through in my mind all the things, "big" or "small" that I felt guilt over. I was amazed at the laundry list of guilt I was holding against myself, going all the way back to when I was a child, stealing one caramel every Saturday afternoon while grocery shopping with my mother! You see, the cubicle mind is a very convincing defense attorney. It has a way of playing with our perceptions of ourselves so that we justify our cubicle ways of thinking and acting thus appearing to avoid the feelings of guilt while guilt is cringing beneath the surface all along!

Here is an example of the everyday operations going on in the courtroom of the cubicle mind.

MEET CRIMINAL DEFENSE ATTORNEY, MS. DEE NILE, CROSS EXAMINING HER CLIENT, MR. GIL TEE.

Mr. Gil Tee, has been accused of sneaking free soft drinks from a local deli by using the smaller, free plastic cups purportedly meant for water and filling them with soda rather than water to avoid paying the price of a regular drink.

Ms. Dee Nile: Mr. Gil Tee, is it true that for the past seven years you have been filling the free plastic cups purportedly meant for water, with soda at "Slices Deli?"

Mr. Gil Tee: Yes, this is true.

Ms. Dee Nile: And Mr. Gil Tee, did you not know the purported purpose of these smaller cups?

Mr. Gil Tee: No maam, I did not. There's not a sign anywhere near the soda fountain or the small cups that states that the purpose of these cups is for water only.

Ms. Dee Nile: So, what you are saying then Mr. Gil Tee, let me be sure I understand you correctly, the merchant had not appropriately labeled the purpose of the small plastic cups, thus you saw them as available for any purpose. Is that correct?

Mr. Gil Tee: Yes maam, that is correct.

Ms. Dee Nile: Mr. Gil Tee, at any time during these past seven years that you have been a regular customer of Slices Deli, did you observe other customers also using the small plastic cups for other things besides water?

Mr. Gil Tee: Oh yes. I witnessed day after day other customers filling those plastic cups with bakery samples, coffee, tea, soda, toothpicks, condiments, straws and even bakery samples to take home. They come with lids you know? I figured customers could use these cups for whatever they wanted. Everybody else was doing it, why shouldn't I?

Ms. Dee Nile: Your honor and ladies and gentlemen of the jury, I think it is quite obvious here that Slices Deli has failed to direct their customers to the appropriate use of their small plastic water cups, and not only is Mr. Gil Tee not guilty of these charges of theft brought against him, but we are suing Slices Deli for the emotional distress and financial setback that this legal battle has brought upon my client. Mr. Gil Tee is an outstanding member of his community and never intended to commit a crime, much less against his favorite deli, Slices.

(Jury goes out to lunch to Slices Deli to deliberate and all 12 use the small plastic water cups for soda instead of purchasing a soft drink with their meal at the counter).

Judge: Has the jury reached a verdict?

Foreman: Yes, your honor we have. We the members of the jury find the defendant, Mr. Gil Tee, "Not Guilty" and grant that the defendant be rewarded one million dollars in damages by the plaintiff, Slices Deli.

After this Mr. Gil Tee patronized another deli and continued his same behavior with the free water cups, never realizing why after every meal he ate there, he experienced heartburn or hiccups or upset stomach or his nose started bleeding. One day he slipped on a small, plastic cup on the floor, broke his nose and sued the new deli who later went out of business due to the financial drain of the lawsuit.

MARY SHARES

Interesting isn't it, how the cubicle heart÷mind craves guilt without admitting to it, like Mr. Gil Tee and how the effects of cubicle guilt run rampant, leading to more guilt ridden behavior. And how the cubicle self justifies its own misbehavior based on other's misbehavior — as we saw in the jury who all skipped out on buying soft drinks by using the water cups.

The point of looking deep within to what we are feeling guilty about is not to declare ourselves guilty and feel bad about ourselves — and maybe some people would think our behaviors in certain areas of our life warrant guilt and others wouldn't — none of that matters.

What matters is how the power of **cubicle guilt** undermines our awareness of our INNOCENCE and our connection to our Inspiring Self Heart∞Mind.

GUILT IS AN OBSTACLE TO PEACE.

Thus, rather than avoiding guilt by justifying our thoughts and behavior with saying things like: "Everyone else does it," "That's the way the world is," "Well, they owe me after all I've done for them," "Everybody thinks that way they just don't admit it, why should I?" and "Oh, it's such a small thing, it's not like I murdered somebody."

Rather than all of this CUBICLE RIGAMAROLE

JUST ADMIT TO YOURSELF THAT YOU
HAVE ENGAGED IN:

Gossiping, lying, stealing, judging, justifying, blaming,
shaming ... you get the picture,

You are feeling guilty about something!

ULTIMATELY, INSPIRATION IS NOT JUDGING US
FOR OUR THOUGHTS, FEELINGS, SENSATIONS OR BEHAVIORS.
THOUGH THERE MAY BE WORLDLY CONSEQUENCES FOR US
TO FACE, INSPIRATION IS NOT PUTTING US ON
TRIAL.

IT IS WAITING FOR US TO ADMIT WHAT WE FEEL GUILTY
ABOUT TO OURSELVES AND

GIVE IT ALL OVER TO INSPIRATION WHO WILL
INFORM US OF WHAT IS REALLY THE TRUTH ABOUT US, THAT

WE ARE INNOCENT.

Some may call this denial. This is incorrect and most
importantly, unhelpful!

To admit to our feelings of guilt and release
them into INSPIRATION so we may experience being set
free, is not denial.

Denial is to not admit our guilt feelings, then
judge ourselves AND OTHERS as guilty and give
ourselves and others a verdict of:

You are sentenced to a lifetime of
guilt –

Without parole!

DENIAL IS NOT KNOWING.
HOW IS GUILT SERVING YOUR RELATIONSHIPS?

NOTICE HOW MANY TIMES A DAY YOU **CONVICT ANOTHER** OF SOME **UNPARDONABLE** BEHAVIOR?

THINGS LIKE:

> **He didn't** take the trash out.
>
> She changed lanes **without** signaling.
>
> **He didn't** return my phone call.
>
> He's five minutes **late**.
>
> She got this invoice **all wrong**.
>
> She **short-changed** me $2.
>
> I saw her eat that banana in the grocery store **before paying for it**.
>
> He **butted in line**.
>
> She's **a flirt**.
>
> He thinks he's a **know it all**.
>
> **What a pity** she has **ruined her life**.
>
> **Who is he kidding** with that outfit?
>
> **Thanks for not** holding the door open for me, mister.
>
> **This isn't** what I ordered. **WHAT A SCREW UP.**
>
> ...

Add your own to the list!

WHAT CAN WE DO INSTEAD?

So, someone cuts in front of you in line at the grocery store.
What now?

NOTICE YOUR REACTION IN THOUGHT, FEELING AND SENSATION.

ADMIT YOUR JUDGMENTS OF THIS PERSON.

ASK YOUR INSPIRED HEART?

"Do I want to condemn this person?"

"Would I condemn myself for this behavior?"

IF YOU ARE LISTENING TO YOUR INSPIRED HEART, THE ANSWER TO BOTH OF THESE QUESTIONS IS "NO!"

If you are listening to the cubicle heart, the answer to both questions is "yes," for **in condemning another, we condemn ourselves.**

To condemn is a **final judgment** on one's **worthiness**.

REMEMBER OUR WORTHINESS? REMEMBER ONE–TO–ONE?

OKAY I HEAR YOU SAYING, "WHAT ABOUT SOMETHING BIGGER THAN THIS — SAY MY SPOUSE OR ANOTHER IS LYING TO ME?

HOW DO I SEE INNOCENCE NOW?"

MARY SHARES

REMEMBER, THE **CUBICLE HEART** ONLY SEES WHAT IT FEELS — **GUILT.**

Notice how someone lying to you brings up guilt in you even though you are not the one doing the lying!

WHY IS THAT?

Because you are judging the lying and judging the person doing the lying; and when we judge another we judge ourselves.

This person has brought up **the cubicle liar** in us! **Never lied, you say?** You just did.

It is the nature of the cubicle heart to lie.

Don't take it personally, just see it for what it is!

DO YOURSELF A FAVOR AND STOP BEING SURPRISED BY THE **CUBICLE HEART÷MIND**.

IT IS WHAT IT IS — THAT IS ALL.

LET INSPIRATION USE IT FOR A HIGHER PURPOSE –

TO BRING YOU INTO AWARENESS OF HOW IN YOUR UNAWARENESS OF THE **CUBICLE SELF**, CUBICLE THOUGHTS ARE RUNNING YOUR LIFE AND STIRRING UP THE POT

AND YOU CAN CHOOSE YOUR

INSPIRING SELF

HEART∞MIND
INSTEAD.

Okay, so what about this lying scoundrel or the murderers and connivers on the evening news?

WHAT ABOUT THEM?

LOOK at WHAT IS BOTHERING YOU about all of these people.

WHY?

so you will RECOGNIZE what is bothering you!

UNTIL YOU DO, YOU WILL FEEL **GUILTY** OR BE **UNAWARE OF FEELING GUILTY** AND YOU WILL **NEVER BE FREE!** **Because you will not feel safe.**

Your Inspiring Heart desires that you feel safe.

BUT THESE PEOPLE NEED TO BE **PUNISHED!**

THERE IS NO PUNISHMENT WORSE THAN ONE'S OWN **GUILTY CONSCIENCE**

AND

Don't worry, we live in a world that will fine or imprison the wrongdoer. There are **in-the-world consequences** for our behavior most of the time.

PAUSE FOR INSPIRATION

What we need to see is that there are in the world consequences to our thoughts!

The **cubicle heart** lies because its thinking is guilty. Its thinking is **guilty** because **it deplores itself. It deplores itself** because **it has no connections — it is experiencing** aloneness.

Admit what you are thinking. Admit your thoughts, feelings, and behaviors, that they may be deplorable or at least not so good — admit it!

INSPIRATION KNOWS THE STATE OF YOUR **CUBICLE HEART** BECAUSE IT KNOWS OF THE **CUBICLE BELIEF IN** ALONE-NESS AND THE **FEAR** THAT GOES WITH IT.

MORE THAN THAT,
IT KNOWS
YOUR INSPIRED
HEART.

EXPERIENCING INNOCENCE
IN YOUR RELATIONSHIPS

••

Pause your mind. Be still on the inside. Still your body if needed.

Express your willingness to open to Inspiration Within; *"I am willing."*

Allow Awareness to shift to Inspiration's Presence within you.

> **Admit** how you have judged yourself and/or another "guilty as charged."

> **Do Not Be Afraid** to feel the guilt. In fact, welcome the guilt so you can be set free from its hold on you.

> **Now, Give it Over.**

Rest with a One-Pointed focus on This Presence. Slow down. Receive.

> **Allow your weariness and the burden of carrying this guilt.** Be relieved in this rest.

> **Open to your Innocence beneath** and let it rise up in you.

> **Be willing to see** this innocence in another who is coming into Your mind right now. Join in your innocence. Rest here.

Listen and Follow This Wisdom revealing Itself to you.

Let go of the outcome.

Give Thanks.

You have Accepted Your Invitation to Innocence.

OPPORTUNITY

INSPIRATION
INSPIRATION
INSPIRATION
INSPIRATION

OPPORTUNITY

∞

INSPIRATION INSPIRES
OPPORTUNITIES.

Opportunities are potential for movement. With every move we make, including our perceptions and actions, we are either moving towards the **cubicle self heart÷mind** or the Inspiring Self Heart∞Mind.

Notice this.

"O" from the **cubicle** perspective stands for **obstacles**.

Do relationships seem like an obstacle course to you?

Are you tired of tripping, falling, climbing, circumventing, avoiding, conflicting, reacting, pushing over, pulling apart, wrestling ... with relationships?

What if that **seeming roadblock** up ahead were seen differently?

What if it were seen as an opportunity or even an adventure to travel into the Land of Inspiration — rather than a **PROJECT** or a **ride into the CUBICLE HALL OF HORRORS**?

How can I see this situation,
this person's behavior or attitude, as an opportunity?

Opportunity for what?

Releasing **cubicle fear** and
experiencing Inspiring
Peace by Being Truly Helpful.

Opportunities bring us face–to–face with our
willingness to trust.

Our walk in the world is a trust walk.

> As I walk in the world in **a heart÷mindset of distrust**, I see opportunities as potential fear — more trouble, more things to do, more of my time and money, sacrifice, loss — some-body, somewhere always wanting more of **me**.

Notice the **"me, me, me."**

As I walk in the world in a Heart∞Mindset of trust, I see opportunities to Be Truly Helpful.

Every relationship is seen as an Opportunity
or an **obstacle!**

EXPERIENCING OPPORTUNITIES
IN YOUR RELATIONSHIPS

When you are experiencing an obstacle in a relationship, whether it is with a store clerk, a family member, friend or life partner, open to practicing the following:

Pause your mind. Be still on the inside. Still your body if needed.

Express your willingness to open to Inspiration Within;
"I am willing."

Allow Awareness to shift to Inspiration's Presence within you.

What is it that you believe to be the obstacle?

What is it that you think you need to happen in this moment?

Now ask, "What do I really want?"

Rest with a One-Pointed focus on This Presence. Slow down. Receive.

In your resting, Say, "I am willing to trust that there is an opportunity behind this seeming obstacle and I open to it now." Stay open to learning something new that will Be Truly Helpful to everyone involved.

Listen and Follow This Wisdom revealing Itself to you.

You may be Guided in ways that surprise you. Perhaps you Will simply let go, see the pettiness of your thinking and/or behavior And walk away, decide not to be offended by another's words and/or Actions, see that you are in no need of defending yourself. What you Do or not do, say or not say is a reflection of your own state of mind: cubicle or Inspired — this is the case for others as well.

Let go of the outcome.

Give Thanks.

You have Accepted Your Invitation

to Opportunities.

NURTURING

INSPIRATION
INSPIRATION
INSPIRATION
INSPIRATION

NURTURING BY OUR TRUE NATURE

∞

INSPIRATION INSPIRES NURTURING BY OUR TRUE NATURE.

Nurturing is meeting and accepting one's True Nature. It is seeing beyond that which is easily seen by the body's eyes, to seeing that which is typically unseen, yet extraordinary. Your True Nature is so beautiful that to behold it is to embrace Life itself; It is the breath that breathes Inspiration and whose Life is eternal spirit.

Imagine if in our relationships of all kinds, we devoted ourselves to nurturing one another's True Nature.

Ah, what gifts we would be and what gifts we would bring to one another in our everyday lives.

Imagine if we were as devoted to our True Nature as we are to our **cubicle nature**.

We would see the world differently.

It would be a different world;

Comforting instead of **attacking**,

Embracing instead of **pushing away**,

Offering instead of **taking**,

Extending instead of **withholding**

and, who knows,

Living instead of **dying**.

Sound idealistic?

Cubicle nature would have us believe
that **the possible is impossible.**

MARY SHARES

I have experienced True Nature days, so I know they are possible.

In fact, they have been my
most productive, joyful days
in the world.

Unlike **the cubicle nature**, our True Nature is quite the creative being and the Spirit of creation
is Prolific, Gifted, Inspiring and never runs out of ideas.

Inspiration shows up when I least expect it,

I get rest and I give with gratitude and receive with a deep sense of absorbing peace.

OUR TRUE NATURE HEALS.

WHEN IS THE LAST TIME YOU FOCUSED ON
DEEPENING YOUR AWARENESS OF YOUR
TRUE NATURE?

HOW DID YOU FEEL?

WHAT THOUGHTS CAME INTO YOUR MIND?

HOW DID YOU RELATE TO OTHERS?

PRACTICE:

Go ahead, right now, ask your

INSPIRING SELF HEART∞MIND,

"What is my True Nature?"

Listen for your answer.

As we attend to being nurtured by our True Nature, we automatically, without thinking, find ourselves being aware of the True Nature in others.

Whether in a smile or passing comment or simply in being present.

Cubicle nature is complicated.

True Nature is simple.

Cubicle nature wants us to believe that Inspiration is complicated, somehow out of reach or doesn't even exist.

In reality, it is so within your reach that you cannot get away from it — no matter what.

No amount of **cubicle thinking** or **behavior** or **ignoring your True Nature** or **denying your True Nature**,

can drive a wedge between you and your True Nature.

That is what makes it True!

Cubicle nature cannot lay a cubicle hand upon it —

no matter what.

It is with you always and
in All Ways.

Nurturing is
meeting one's
True Nature
and saying,
"YES."

EXPERIENCING our TRUE NATURE in our relationships

Pause your mind. Be still on the inside. Still your body
if needed.

Express your willingness to open to Inspiration Within;
"I am willing."

Allow Awareness to shift to Inspiration's Presence within you.

Envision a relationship whose True Nature is
calling out to you.

Yes, relationships have a cubicle nature and a True
Nature, Inspired Nature.

One relationship has already entered your mind.
See it in all of Its cubicle strife and strain. Do not be
afraid, **BE WILLING. Remain anchored
to Inspiration Within.**

Rest with a One-Pointed focus on This Presence.
Slow down. Receive.

Now, allow Inspiration Within to show you
your Inspired Self.

Now, see your Inspired Self meeting the other
person's Inspired Self, True Nature.

What are you experiencing now?

Rest in the Flow of Nurturing Spirit.

Listen and Follow This Wisdom revealing Itself to you.

Let go of the outcome.

Give Thanks.

You have Accepted Your Invitation to

Deepening Your Awareness

of Your True Nature

and Another's True Nature.

CONCLUSION

ALREADY FREE

Inspiration is longing to Inspire us — Let It.

Inspiration desires to Inspire our relationships — Let It.

How is Love revealing Love to you?

Are you pausing?

Are you listening?

Are you responding?

It is your pausing, listening and responding to Inspiration Within that is Being Truly Helpful in all of your relationships.

This is the communication that heals, because this is the communication that joins.

Ah, to be willing to let Inspiration Inspire my desires through my willingness to be fulfilled —

To be free, in the peace of Inspiration.

HINT:

It is already happening.

You are already free.

Pause for Inspiration

Be Willing to Receive.

Listen.

Respond.

Follow Inspiration

∞

∞

∞

Now,

Give Thanks.